COLORS OF FILM

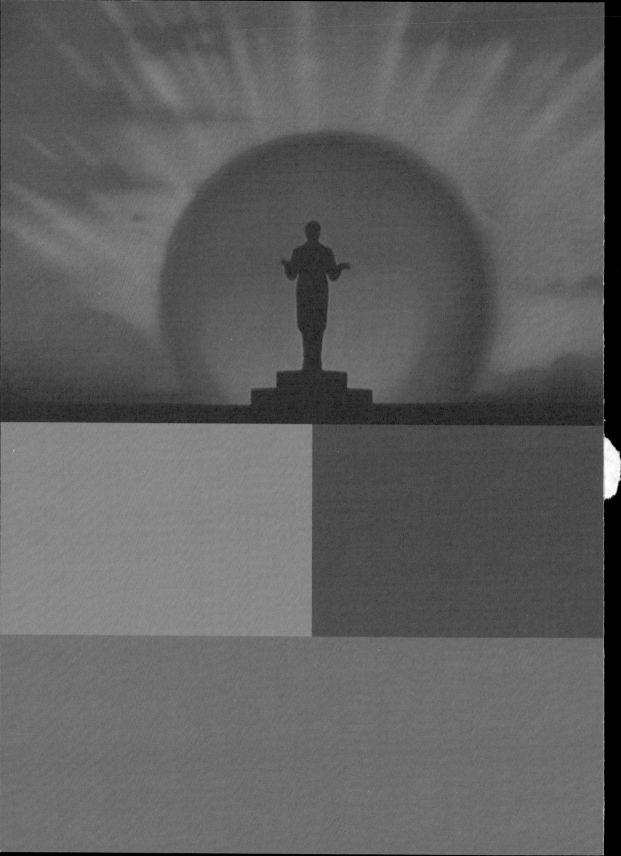

COLORS OF FILM

THE STORY OF CINEMA IN 50 PALETTES

Charles Bramesco

FRANCES
LINCOLN

CONTENTS

for Maddie,
without whom my
world would be
monochrome

INTRODUCTION

Cinema is not set in stone. No aspect of the medium is completely immutable, least of all color. Dialogue can be bleeped or re-dubbed, and soundtracks can be swapped in or out to accommodate music licensing rights. Plot can be chopped up by the almighty rewind and fast-forward buttons, or by the hordes of autodidact video editors cutting together fan tributes on YouTube and social media. Reformatting a film for broadcast on TV, home-video release, or aeroplane seatback screens can stretch the aspect-ratio rectangle to haunted-house-mirror proportions. But the change in color is all but inevitable, a function of time's onward march rather than deliberate creative intervention.

    If not properly tended, a filmstrip will fade or be subject to other discoloration, as its blacks turn maroon or a wash of red tints the frame. In the movie theaters designed to set the standard for technical presentation, incorrect lensing on the projector can dim the brightness, not so differently from the warming and cooling color settings on a TV. Computerized storage doesn't guarantee fidelity either—the processes of screenshotting and jpeg-pasting as susceptible to deterioration as physical preservation. Digital projection will not produce the same texture and hue as its analogue forebears on 35mm reels or the bigger and bolder 70mm; which of them can be said to be the true color of the work at hand?

Type any search for a specific shot into Google—"door scene Titanic" provides a shared frame of reference for us all—and you'll find an array of color-warped versions of the same image. Jack clings to Rose as he sinks into the icy Atlantic, a navy blue filter overlaid to communicate the sub-zero temperatures. In another, the light levels on the dark blues have been turned up so that we might luxuriate in every last detail of a young Leonardo DiCaprio's face. Another result does away with the blue entirely, highlighting the off-white and cream tones in Jack's shirt and Rose's lifejacket. Keep scrolling, and a saturated version plays up the red of Rose's hair, a storybook luster to go with the impossible romance. After no more than a few minutes, it gets harder to recall which one is "right": the one you remember from the endless theatrical run or the two-cassette VHS set you had in your youth. With enough distance from experience, memory becomes the final stage of recoloring.

A fickle, indefinite thing, color, and yet a crucial one. A well-placed red or green can dictate tone or plant symbolic meaning, establish a location or time (both for the setting and the period of its real-world production), identify characters as heroes or villains. We can chart shifting social mores in the gradually purpling hue of prop blood, or the contrast of light on Black actors' skin. The book in your hands proffers an incomplete survey of all that color can do and be in cinema, approaching the topic both as a concept deployed in the artistic process and as a tangible quantity fabricated by professionals at the forefront of their fields. Tackling such a broad subject requires a combination of technical explication to break down the nitty-gritty answers to the question of how, deep-tissue criticism to get to the heart of why, and cohesive history to put it all together in the context of an ongoing narrative. The evolution of color is the evolution of cinema itself—an equipment-forward business, an art form, and an extension of the society creating it.

   Color lends itself to an uncommonly linear story in the way each revolutionary advance supplants the last one. This book's four sections have been divided up along these lines, with the first part taking us from the inception of moving pictures to the heyday of Technicolor, the second running up to Technicolor's demise, the third addressing the videotape era, and the fourth sifting through the mass digitization that brings us to the present. We can see other global developments playing out within this framework, as cheapening film stock brought color cinematography to emergent national movements, while competition between consumer-grade giants Kodak and Fujifilm gave amateurs state-of-the-art tools. Color provides a ready bellwether for change on the macrocosmic level, each new breakthrough of brilliance reflected in a look unique to its moment.

   Even within something as subtle and aesthetically pure as color, there's still an embedded politics, sometimes explicit and sometimes buried in subtext. A genius in his final days adopts blue as a figurative and literal way of seeing the world, as well as an act of protest; a queer satire mocks retro notions of femininity by turning up the pink until it's garish enough to serve as a parody of itself; in a developing Senegal, the tension between local heritage and colonialist interference plays out in the contrast between organic and manmade colors. Cinema deals in visual information, with reams of commentary and subjectivity encoded in curtains, a shirt, or other unobtrusive detritus of the everyday. Color is the perfect hiding place for significance, most powerful when left unstated.

But for all its versatility as metaphor, color can also be a presence unto itself, as expressive and tactile as any actor. Avant-garde cinema and the mainstream relatives sampling its hallucinatory un-logic may place swirls of abstract color in place of character and dialogue, overriding storytelling and going straight to visceral building of a mood. For this, we may have Walt Disney to partially thank, his finest hour being a feature-length tribute to the raw magnificence of color and sound in its most unadulterated form. He saw that color wasn't just one more way to make the light dancing on the silver screen closer to reproducing our sense of sight, but an infinitely malleable force that can be translated to violence, disorientation, or love.

On relevance over bottom-line quotient of genius, we've compiled a curriculum of fifty films that attempt to explore the full potential of color, both in spectrum and application. Although I personally must cop to a somewhat Hollywood-centric mindset as an American, the titles selected for this book were chosen for variety, straining to cover the full breadth of the medium across nations, eras, genres, industry scale, and subject matter. With one notable exception, black and white films have been excluded for lack of pertinence and the sake of organization, although another book could be written on the painterly interplay of light and shadow that makes up a monochrome composition. To this same effect,

we could easily have rounded up fifty documentaries
raising an entirely different set of philosophical enquiries,
a conversation too rich and dense to be confined to
one or two picks.

Within this curriculum, groups of films may be cognitively
lumped together to form miniature lesson plans. A trio of
clown-colored musicals spanning the Atlantic Ocean and
the better part of a century collectively illustrate how influence
begets homage and deconstruction. The digital age section can
be boiled down to three action epics—one favoring practical
effects, one all computerized, and one an innovative mix of
both—in which heroes zip around futuristic landscapes at
breakneck speeds in souped-up vehicles too rad to be real.
An essential 1950s melodrama gains a companion piece in a
loose remake twenty years later. Two portraits of tormented
womanhood use radically dissimilar palettes to make
comparable statements about the hardships of compulsory
heterosexuality. Ideally, the chronological arrangement of the
entries will build an expanding bank of knowledge that primes
cinephiles and lay readers alike to digest each successive
chapter, and with time, each new film they watch.

More than to inform, the goal of this book is to spark curiosity
in something that even lifelong movie-watchers can take for
granted. Just as I was changed by the time spent writing this,
I hope readers will also come out the other side of this project
unable to look at any footage without stopping to consider the
precise brown of that tree, or why that wall has been painted
such a deep shade of yellow. Or, to go one better, that they'll
also give whatever that evening's programming might be a
cursory search online to learn about the color choices; one
of my major takeaways from the research stage was that every
film's coloration has a backstory in the collaboration between

directors and production designers, hair stylists, costumers, and cinematographers, all working together while expressing their own sensibility. This change in perspective might even carry over to reality as we grow more observant and critical of the intentionality behind the color we see in advertising, packaging, architecture, and anything else we might encounter on a walk down the street.

Color is joy, energy, life itself. With the right machines and chemicals, and a little inspiration, film can take us anywhere and show us anything. In Michael Powell and Emeric Pressburger's war fantasy *A Matter of Life and Death*, an inter-dimensional guide steps out of the celestial Other World and back into ours, announcing his arrival with a sigh: "Up there, one is starved for Technicolor." Even in heaven, they envy the beauty of the cinema. Down here, movie obsessives act much the same, whiling away the workdays until we can feel that vivid rush one more time. We're starved, too. This book is the beginning of a feast. Turn the page and dig in.

OVER THE RAINBOW

A poster for *The Miracle*, the world's first full-color narrative.

In the beginning, there was nothingness. And then there was light—the movie projector making photographs dance on an illuminated wall as if by magic. The development of the earliest film-based motion picture technology, improving on the optical illusion of the spinning zoetrope's GIF-like repetitions, fell in line with an impulse dating back to the dawn of the human species to shrink the distance between real life and our visual representations of it. Photography one-upped painting with as-you-see-it literalism; cinema did one better by suspending its snatches of time in a half-state both moving and frozen; and now virtual reality nips at the art form's heels. The inexorable introduction of color to the equation posed an odd conundrum, inching closer to the ideal of total realism by adding elements not necessarily present in the scene. However unrefined, the first works in color put forth an early example of cinema's power to make deft falseness feel truer than the truth.

But in the heady days of color film's beginnings, the most pressing concerns were practical, not philosophical. The industry leaders knew full well that they needed to catch up with the range of color that painting had enjoyed for centuries if the movies were to transcend their limited reputation as a nifty curiosity and be accepted as a fully-fledged fine art. A great many tried their hand at mass-producing color film, all of them facing the same roadblock that—no matter the approach—it would take a great deal of time, money, and expertize. They were sure there had to be a faster path than a warehouse full of professionals carefully painting by hand, if only they could figure it out.

An arms race broke out as dozens of operations scrambled to perfect and patent their own colorization processes, each still visible as an overlay on black and white film. Segundo de Chomón, the leading light of silent-era Spain, trademarked a stencilling procedure using velvet rollers soaked in dye while working in Spain for the Pathé brothers. What would be copyrighted as Pathéchrome brought the world the first full-color narrative feature film, *The Miracle* (1912), and the technique reigned supreme until employees at Famous Players-Lasky (a decade from the studio tacking Paramount onto its name) coined the similar yet sufficiently different Handschiegl process in 1916. Kodak threw its hat into the ring with Sonochrome, a pre-tinted film with attention-grabbing names like Peachblow, Purplehaze, and Fleur de lis.

The various tints and dyes left something to be desired; these were the attempts of mere mortals at approximating reality, not the actual colors themselves. "Natural color" was the next peak to be scaled, and the first to reach the summit was the British one-time hypnotist George Albert Smith. His homemade Kinemacolor used red and green filters both in front of the camera's shutter and the projector's lens to capture the partial coloration of a scene, reduced to those two hues. Prizma would carry this concept further with bipack color sandwiching two different emulsions on a single roll of film, gaining in clarity and brightness. (The term "two-strip," often used interchangeably with bipack, is a misnomer in this respect.)

Technicolor threw their hat into the ring with bipack Kodachrome in 1915, a name the company would recycle for its unrelated, better-known multicolor stock later in the century. It wasn't until 1932 that they'd finally break through to the complete spectrum of color with three-strip technology. (This one actually *did* use multiple strips.) The belt-tightening of the Great Depression ensured that two-color film would stick around as a low-cost alternative, and that black and white film would remain commonplace for filmmakers who preferred its economical expressiveness. But audiences' eyes had been opened, and they refused to go back. It wasn't long before "In Glorious Technicolor!" grew from an adman's idiom for trailers and posters to a guarantee of the highest quality.

Every film restoration effort comes bundled with a minor existential quandary: in spiffing up an older work, might we be losing something integral along the way? Fans cherish a title like *Night of the Living Dead* (George A. Romero, 1968) in no small part due to the scuzz factor, and scrubbing clean a beat-up print would be to remove it of its endearing grubbiness and its personality. With this in mind, the team working on that film's ultra-sharp 4K treatment back in 2016 were keen to hold on to what they called the "pimples" that make Romero's zombie genre-definer the treasure it is. Perhaps they trod so gently because that film had already been the subject of a kerfuffle in cinephile circles some decades earlier, for undergoing a similar process that had exponentially exacerbated these very issues.

The post-facto colorization of black and white motion pictures has long drawn controversy, chiefly from purists who see it as plain and simple tampering. As computer programming boomed in the early 1980s, blotting color onto a filmstrip was streamlined to a matter of clicks for companies like Colorization, Inc., far removed from the exhausting tribulation of Élisabeth Thuillier's day. Second-tier outfit Hal Roach Studios was among the first to commission "modernized" versions of their library, as well as works in the public domain like *Night of the Living*

Dead. But cinephiles cried foul against the blown-out pastels defiling their graven text, in particular the pea-soup skin tone applied to the zombies, the clearest evidence that the colorization team had made creative decisions not included within the work itself.

Their complaints fell in line with a pushback lodged at the highest levels of Hollywood by artists championing the intrinsic value of black and white, a coalition including Woody Allen, George Lucas, and Billy Wilder. (In a special episode of their long-running TV show, critics Roger Ebert and Gene Siskel decried this trend as a "new vandalism.") They contended that the finer points of film production differ wildly between monochrome and colored shooting, that everything from lighting designs to costuming can't be changed so drastically without losing touch with the creators' vision. It didn't help that many of these conversions took place without the consent of the director; Frank Capra had signed on to co-produce a colored version of *It's a Wonderful Life* (1946), but when the Colorization, Inc. executives realized that they didn't legally require his assistance and cut him out, he swore off the process as a scourge forever.

Lawsuits abounded during this period, many of them sent in the direction of TV mogul Ted Turner, who spearheaded the campaign to slap a fresh coat of paint

POST-FACTO COLORIZATION

Colorized First World War footage from Peter Jackson's *They Shall Not Grow Old.*

on the past. His Turner Entertainment conglomerate acquired MGM's catalogue of over two-thousand films and went to work milking every last broadcasting dollar from them with hasty colorizations, his most egregious eyesore a desecrated *Casablanca* (Michael Curtiz, 1942). He and other proponents branded this as an inevitable update that would reignite public interest in stale classics, although Turner's comments at a 1986 fundraiser made the case more frankly: "The last time I checked, I owned the films that we're in the process of colorizing. I can do whatever I want with them, and if they're going to be shown on television, they're going to be in color."

The widespread hostility to colorization has mostly relegated it to niche projects in the vein of Peter Jackson's *They Shall Not Grow Old* (2018), a compilation of recovered First World War field footage. Nevertheless, protecting the integrity of images has become a more urgent proposition than ever as media literacy comes under attack from bad-faith operators spewing deepfakes and fake news onto the internet. Interference in color may seem less overtly dangerous, but just consider the insidious lightening or darkening of skin as one sign of the sway these processes hold. If red can be made blue and dark can be made light, there's no limit to the deceptions that can be snuck into mass communication.

SHOOTING FOR THE STARS

A TRIP TO THE MOON
GEORGES MÉLIÈS 1902

Georges Méliès didn't make pictures move, but it could be said that he dreamt up the concept of the "movie." He was the first to bottle all the transportive handmade wonder the term now implies, pushing a nascent narrative form to far-off planets never seen before. The French stage prestidigitator's greatest trick was to take the cinema and imbue it with his cunning brand of magic, coining much of the visual vocabulary still in use today, from the dissolve to the multiple exposure to fun with spliced screens. His most well-known short and silent film, *A Trip to the Moon*, shoots a cadre of astronomers with names like Parafaragaramus into orbit via a bullet-shaped vessel that wedges itself in the moon's winking eye, a neat impression of Méliès' impish comedic sensibility and an iconic image invoked dozens of times over the following century. The enshrinement of that sight gag in the cinematic canon speaks to the film's incalculable impact on the medium it helped codify, but fate would still toy with its legacy for decades to come.

In this early stage of film's infancy, colorization was a painstaking procedure conducted by hand in the laboratory of the unsung trailblazer Élisabeth Thuillier, career-long colorist to Méliès. She regimented her two hundred or so specialists in a drawn-out assembly line that tasked each artist with painting one color directly onto the film stock with a brush, a crude method that still combined as many as twenty different base colors in a single reel. Although black and white copies were somewhat easier to find, color versions were extremely rare: Thuillier's lab was said to have produced only sixty color prints in total, making them a collector's item eventually believed extinct. However, in 1993, a bulk donation to a Spanish film archive yielded one such elusive gem, which then required twelve years of careful restoration before it could be shown.

Except this wasn't Thuillier's handiwork, but a second-generation print with one subtle yet telling detail altered: a waving flag had been painted in the colors of Spain, suggesting that the extant print had been intended for Spanish exhibition. This footnote serves as a twofold lesson, not just illustrating that colorizing is as autonomous and vital a piece of post-production as editing or sound, but also that even a small splash of dye can fundamentally change the meaning of a text. Thuillier's passing soon ended her collaboration with Méliès, her laboratory left to the daughter she'd trained in the family business. But long after her name receded into textbooks, her alchemical breakthroughs continued to guide countless indirect disciples.

● #D4746B
R212 G116 B107

● #8DB657
R141 G182 B87

● #CB5333
R203 G83 B51

EPIC PROPORTIONS

INTOLERANCE
D.W. GRIFFITH
1916

In 1915, *The Birth of a Nation* and its lionization of the Ku Klux Klan, director D.W. Griffith left a stain on the cinematic canon while incurring condemnation from the National Association for the Advancement of Colored People (NAACP) and many others opposed to its deep-seated racism. He intended his follow-up, *Intolerance*, as rebuttal, not cowed apology—proof that he could muster compassion and open-heartedness with the best of them. Significantly, the silent film would address this theme in broad historical terms and leave the question of Blackness out of it, instead weaving a grand tapestry between four narratives in four periods: a clash in ancient Babylon, a retelling of Christ's crucifixion, the St Bartholomew's Day massacre in Renaissance France, and a crime-and-punishment melodrama in then-contemporary America. Enlightened standards for moral decency would cast his efforts in a less flattering light, but the staggering scope of Griffith's vision ensured it landmark status.

In the silent era, everything from facial overacting to linear editing was geared for clear communication to an audience that had only just learned how to watch a movie. Griffith marshalled color along these same lines, using whole-frame tinting to distinguish each interwoven narrative thread from the others. (Unlike dyeing by hand, tinting involved immersing the frames into a chemical solution that would soak into the photographic emulsion and leave a stain in a tone of the artist's choosing. Kodak would launch sales of pre-tinted stock in 1921.) In the original version, Babylon appeared in a greyish green, the life and times of Jesus were set in blue, the French material was sepia, and the twentieth century glowed orange, although some currently available prints of his film have lost the one-to-one color-coding to re-dyeing.

The assigned colors don't adhere to a perceptible logic beyond separation from one another, but other films following his example relied on connotative associations (romantic scenes in magenta, ruddy browns for desert-set Westerns) or visual imitation (darker blues stood in for night-time, square one for "day for night" shooting). Griffith cast the burning of Georgia scene in *The Birth of a Nation* in scorching red, another reflection of his ceaseless impulse to develop the capabilities of a primitive cinema. In his later years, he'd design a rig of lights, which would be installed within cinemas and flash at different sections of the screen. Impractical, sure, but his restless inventiveness still paved the way for the pie-in-the-sky contraptions of James Cameron and Christopher Nolan.

 #DD966C
R221 G150 B108 #6D3726
R109 G55 B38

NOT IN KANSAS ANYMORE

THE WIZARD OF OZ
VICTOR FLEMING
1939

Bored farm girl Dorothy Gale experiences a provincial daily life in Kansas in shades of sepia, evoking the dustiness of vintage photography and silent films that Hollywood had only just advanced beyond. The dreary dullness of her surroundings compels her to retreat into fantasy, a dream sequence where a twister sends her tumbling into the merry old land of Oz. There, the scenery is bathed in saturated hues by the new processing technique called three-strip Technicolor, after the way in which it captured a rich spectrum by layering three colored filmstrips on top of one another. Although the system had not yet been perfected—to achieve the colors' dazzle required extremely bright lighting, which raised temperatures on set to a sweltering 100°F and allegedly gave some of the extras permanent eye damage—the results were too beautiful to be argued with.

The depth of color in three-strip Technicolor was unlike anything moviegoers had seen up to that point, a miracle that the production team recognized in advance. The script from Noel Langley, Florence Ryerson, and Edgar Allan Woolf accentuated the color-specific aspects of L. Frank Baum's original story, changing Dorothy's silver footwear from the source text into Judy Garland's iconic ruby slippers to match the vibrancy of the Yellow Brick Road and Emerald City.

In the shot opposite, the first glimpse we get of the gleaming citadel on a hill along with our pack of adventurers, it's instantly clear why naming the place "Green City" wouldn't have sufficed. The choice of gemstones as stand-ins for colors communicates a brilliance rarer than the commonplace or everyday, the precise glamour that Dorothy—and audiences—left home in search of.

By 1939, the American public's morale had been ground down by a decade of economic deprivation starting with the Great Depression, and the cinema rose to prominence as a cheap source of populist entertainment. Dorothy's imagined odyssey through this glittery wonderland provides her with the same escapist pleasure that ordinary folks looked for in a night out at the movies, even if that respite from the drudgery of reality lasts no longer than a couple hours. The genius of Victor Fleming's film comes from its inspired artifice; the Emerald City the gang sees is actually a matte painting by pioneering behind-the-scenes artist Warren Newcombe, inserted via a doubly exposed composite shot, its jewel tones too magnificent to be true.

 #7C9987
R124 G153 B135

 #CDA243
R205 G162 B67

● #6A6C4C
R107 G108 B76

#C9B7A6
R201 G183 B166

#453417
R69 G52 B23

THE WIZARD'S SORCERY

FANTASIA
WALT DISNEY PRODUCTIONS 1940

The Golden Age studio bosses looked down on Walt Disney's animation house as small fry cranking out kids' stuff, but his productions enjoyed certain freedoms inaccessible to Jack Warner and the others. Cartoons were unburdened by actors, sets, or the basic laws of nature, limited only by what the elite ranks of animators could cook up. If stuffy grown-ups refused to take animation seriously, the Mouse House would show them all, plotting a highbrow masterpiece meant to display the properties unique to an underestimated corner of cinema. Announcing his aspirations to greatness by surrounding himself with it (the opening narration defines Fantasia as "a new form of entertainment"), Disney selected compositions from such luminaries as Bach, Beethoven, and Stravinsky, then put his underpaid underlings to work on eye-popping accompaniments. Mickey gets into misadventures with the living brooms, an elegant ballet cycles through the seasons, and a celestial clash pits demonic evil against light-bearing monks.

Before all that, Disney's first order of business was to familiarize his viewers with both the orchestra itself and the creative philosophy under which it would operate. The "Toccata and Fugue in D Minor" segment tidily accomplishes both, explaining its principle of art appreciation for its own sake through what narrator Deems Taylor calls "absolute music," melodies unshackled by any plot or even concrete mental imagery. After some live-action shots introducing conductor Leopold Stokowski and the individual instrument sections with gel-filtered footlights casting towering shadows, the studio melts away and we drift into the hand-drawn plane. Shimmers of amorphous color glide across formless vistas, landscapes without the land. With no narrative to get in the way, an undeveloped brain can focus itself on the traits of color: luster, intensity, and other visual qualities an infant can giggle at before they can speak.

This segment sets the scene for the film that follows as a thesis statement of sorts: a declaration that color and sound in its most unadulterated form wield an emotive power immediate enough for even a child to tap into. Freed from a storyline or characters to cement intent, with the music offering the only prompt toward mood, Disney demonstrated that a sickly yellow can connote unease on an instinctual level. Cartoon sceptics knocked his chipper early shorts for a perceived juvenile streak, doodles trading formal maturity for comic-strip chuckles; however, for his self-styled magnum opus, he winnowed away everything until mastery was the only element remaining, a work of true art under the strictest definition of the term. With that much proven, he then built an empire on the idea that that artistry needn't be sacrificed in catering to younger viewers.

#363248
R54 G50 B72

#4A504F
R74 G80 B79

#C9AE81
R200 G174 B130

CASTLE ON A CLOUD

BLACK NARCISSUS
MICHAEL POWELL & EMERIC PRESSBURGER 1947

The sacred flirts with the profane in the most ravishingly lush entry within Powell and Pressburger's estimable body of work. A flock of Protestant nuns set a course for a derelict convent high in the Indian Himalayas, where the mission to set up a hospital and school for the secluded area tests their religious resolve. Everything conspires to undermine their vows of self-discipline and self-deprivation, starting with the sensuous grandeur of the mountain range splayed around the palace that has been repurposed as the sisters' quarters. Although production never strayed out of the venerable Pinewood Studios in England, a combination of Academy Award-winning sets by Alfred Junge, expressionistic cinematography from Jack Cardiff, and astonishing matte paintings by W. Percy Day harnessed the exhilarating sweep of the high-altitude setting.

The Technicolor bounty of the rolling green hills, the ornate Darjeeling attire, even the juicy tomatoes the nuns dare not eat—all strike a contrast with the crisp, pressed, off-white habits ("the color of oatmeal," as Powell put it) worn in line with their ascetic denial of fleshly pleasure. The film theorist Kristin Thompson has singled out the color blue as the key motif, its decadence a counter to the upheld ideal of cloistered purity. During a prayer, one sister finds her gaze drifting to the window, and the leafy branch wobbling against a cerulean sky; while planting hearty, modest potatoes, another can't help gazing out toward the inviting, frost-topped peaks. A pivotal exchange plays out in a deeper-blue chamber, its walls embellished with erotic drawings hinting at the room's past use as a harem. In one nun's flashback to her pre-conversion days, she wears a cornflower gown as she prepares for a wedding that won't happen.

The most striking distraction from Christ's work comes in the form of a strapping, shorts-wearing emissary overseeing operations for the area's commanding general. Unbidden carnal desires gradually overtake the women, their abstinent repression exploding into madness that seeps into the palette of the film. After renouncing the order, one nun reappears in a dress of come-hither maroon, and the setting sun drowns other scenes in a radiant orange. In reaching the hallucinatory intensity of the final act, Powell and Pressburger defied the regulations set by Technicolor's "Color Consultant" Natalie Kalmus to enforce a standardized visual profile for all films made with the company's technology. The swells of raw hunger for life spilling out onto the screen looked unlike anything else, just how Powell and Pressburger wanted it.

#9F9883
R159 G152 B131

#7D4B34
R125 G75 B52

#9EC6AB
R158 G199 B171

#C0C2C1
R192 G194 B193

#9F5759
R159 G87 B89

#656E84
R101 G110 B132

#484534
R72 G69 B53

#9C5834
R156 G88 B52

#886D66
R136 G108 B101

HOLLYWOOD'S INDIAN HOLIDAY

THE RIVER
JEAN RENOIR
1951

At the time of its production, the top dogs at Technicolor considered the photography on Jean Renoir's first color film to be the best use of their materials yet. The filmmaker Éric Rohmer later agreed, calling it "the most beautiful color we have ever seen on screen." French film criticism godhead André Bazin went one step further, declaring that this wasn't just the most beautiful color film ever made, but almost "the first one," which "erases even our memory of black-and-white film." Martin Scorsese recalls a boyhood screening as one of the road-to-Damascus epiphanies that put him on the path to a career in cinema, and still counts it as a favorite to this day. (He and his non-profit The Film Foundation would prove instrumental in a 2004 restoration effort.)

Its lofty standing in the canon belies the humility of Renoir's on-location excursion to India, the Western viewing public's first chance to see the faraway land through Technicolor goggles. Far from the safari of tigers and elephants that Renoir's producers in Hollywood asked for when he told them he wanted to adapt the novel by author Rumer Godden (who also wrote *Black Narcissus*), the film instead trains its focus on the human and spiritual dimensions of life in a pre-independence Kolkata. The British owner of a jute mill raises his son and five daughters in a progressive fusion of Christian and Hindu belief systems, rooted in a deference to the culture of his adopted home. Renoir, with assistance from virtuoso-to-be of Indian cinema Satyajit Ray, sought to adopt that same consciousness in his stylistic brushstrokes.

In the much-trumpeted color, Renoir's aim to show English speakers a more grounded India is juxtaposed with the vibrancy that the Caucasian imagination thought of as part and parcel of the exotic. The dyed wares at the local bazaar, the pigmented dust flung during the Holi festival, and a brief fantasy in which a bride and groom morph into deities all put the Technicolor through its paces. But these flourishes punctuate a more dialled-back naturalism emphasizing the scenery familiar to the average villager: the pale greens of the sun-parched grasslands, the ruddy bricks laid centuries earlier, the flowing milk-chocolate tides of the Ganges through which all metaphysical energy surges. Renoir's good intention to blend in with his setting can sometimes amount to a change in "flavor," a word used in the opening narration to ease the presumed viewer into a foreign story working within a literary form they already knew. But in toting his camera to the subcontinent, he went where none of his cohort had gone before.

#DEBA60
R222 G186 B96

#5D6576
R93 G101 B118

#C36250
R195 G98 B80

#CA5A4E
R202 G90 B78

#657DB1
R101 G125 B177

#625036
R98 G80 B54

#D1B99B
R209 G185 B155

GOTTA DANCE, GOTTA DANCE

SINGIN' IN THE RAIN
STANLEY DONEN & GENE KELLY
1952

The American entertainment industry has never been shy about mythologizing itself, usually with a trace of aggrandizement, and this self-referential seriousness is punctured in hilarious fashion by the wicked wit of Stanley Donen's seminal satire. Metro-Goldwyn-Mayer had carved itself a nice market share on the strength of the musicals churned out at an efficient clip under producer Arthur Freed's unit, the same moviemaking milieu skewered with inside-baseball precision in their high-watermark triumph. As the movie biz makes the changeover from silence to sound in the late 1920s, opportunity calls for a star clinging to his celebrity, a below-the-line music man and a wannabe A-lister hoping to break in, all of them united by their undying love of the work. Like the film around them, they're in thrall to the thrills and the glitz inherent in putting on a show—the same passion that led to the old saying about a bad day on set beating a good day anywhere else.

Donen and his co-director and star Gene Kelly understood that flashy production numbers could convey this intoxicating excitement more effectively than anything else, and used the song-and-dance sequences as a walking tour through a lampooned yet romanticized Hollywood. The most deliriously virtuosic scene instead pays tribute to the stage, a pressure-cooker crucible for performers where no one gets a second take to move their audience to laugh or weep. The "Broadway Melody" riffs on the musical theater trope of the dream ballet, in which the characters' inner turmoils and euphorias transcend language and burst out through the body's motion; in this instance, the multi-phase showcase for Kelly's talents happens to be in the form of a movie pitch about a hoofer in flapper-era New York.

Through a hullabaloo at a speakeasy interrupted by gangsters and a stunning pas de deux redefining the term "infinity scarf," the Technicolor reds, greens, and yellows portray Broadway as a playland of exuberant fakery, its colors bewitching not in spite of their unnatural pop, but because of it. The grand finale breaks back into song as a tuxedoed Kelly and the ensemble dash onto a minimalist soundstage lit by the metropolitan constellation of lightbulb-lined signs around Manhattan. It's a manmade firmament of stars, the blinking lights a canny shorthand for the sparkle that can only come from artisans' skilled labor. Some hues are too bright to be found in the wild, so we have no choice but to forge them ourselves.

 #484981
R72 G73 B129

#C74846
R199 G72 B70

 #221300
R34 G19 B0

 #E6C657
R230 G198 B87

#B099A5
R176 G153 B165

#DDEBE8
R221 G235 B232

MOVING PICTURES

ALL THAT HEAVEN ALLOWS
DOUGLAS SIRK
1955

There are those who think of "melodrama" as a dirty word, a pejorative reserved for films with rafter-rattling overacting and exaggerated contrivances of plot. But "melo" comes from the Greek *melos* meaning "song," as in melody, and suggests a more lyrical, florid slant on run-of-the-mill realism. In the few—career-defining—melodramas made by Douglas Sirk during the 1950s, he deals in a pathos onto which anyone can project themselves and their own private heartbreaks. He only loses the melodrama sceptics in his choice to bring everything else up to this overheated temperature, the emotive lighting and set design carrying the emotions on the verge of bubbling over. In the exquisite *All That Heaven Allows*, as the fetching widow Cary resigns herself to the grim likelihood that she'll never find another love, the flaming yellow-orange foliage of the New England autumn outside withers into the numbing blue of winter.

Sirk makes no bones about the barely underlying symbolism of his colors, but then, the feelings they stand in for are hardly quiet. For her WASPy neighbors' stuffy soirée, Cary pours herself into a va-va-voom scarlet dress, sending the message that she's still in her sexual prime to potential suitors loud and clear. She takes a liking to Ron, the dreamboat arborist who's been flirting up a storm with her, much to the murmuring consternation of her judgemental neighbors and selfish grown-up children. The couple's disparity in age and class falls away as they kindle a mutually smoldering *affaire de coeur*; the roaring fire in Ron's self-made woodland bachelor cabin fills it with the same snuggly orange seen around the hearth in Cary's living room.

In the buttoned-up, upper-crust setting of Stoningham, people can only show their true colors in a very literal way. Cary's college-educated daughter Kay tries her best to support her mother's choices, but ultimately succumbs to pressure from her cattier peers. Her ambivalence comes streaming through the window above her bed as multicolor, casting an inexplicable jumbled rainbow of light across her body. Cary and Ron's color scheme isn't so fractured, best summed up in the final shot's powerful contrast of their indoor love nest's nurturing warm tones against the cold and lonely outdoors from which they're taking shelter. Technicolor added visual kerosene to the heat of this furtive romance, every soft-focus close-up of the preternaturally telegenic Jane Wyman and Rock Hudson woozy with wanting. Sirk's emotionality was so scaldingly intense that many critics couldn't see past it. A generation of reappraisal and reclamation would revise our view of his works, now hailed not as weepy women's pictures, but as luxuriant symphonies of household agony and ecstasy.

 #588FB5
R88 G143 B181

#66362C
R102 G54 B44

 #493114
R73 G49 B20

HOME ON THE RANGE

THE SEARCHERS
JOHN FORD
1956

A rugged, outdoorsman self-sufficiency has been part of the United States' cultural DNA since covered wagons first blazed a path to the Pacific, but it's because of John Ford that we can still picture it today. The great outdoors was his studio, and the sky, soil, and rivers filled his box of paints. As the unrivalled king of the Western, he's had a greater hand than any other single filmmaker in solidifying the public's image of the rough-and-tumble frontier, its untamed majesty in need of wrestling into civilization by hard-bitten men. *The Searchers* has settled into the consensus choice for his magnum opus, for considering the mournful personal cost exacted by that storied duty, with the usual cowboy played by John Wayne exposed as a broken, hateful, obsolete old man. Throughout this sobering reassessment of Wild West machismo, however, Ford could never deny the lure of the terrain they'd come to conquer.

Some viewers approach the Ford filmography as travelogue, his extensive Great Plains location shooting a seated cruise through the most breathtaking sights the country has to offer. A forbidding stretch of desert located on the Utah–Arizona line in the Navajo Nation's reservation, Monument Valley became his stomping ground across ten productions and provided a handful of other filmmakers with a backdrop of nature's gritty splendor. On the grassless expanses trod by Wayne's bitter gunslinger Ethan Edwards as he retrieves a kidnapped daughter, the world is reduced to two bands of color: the burnt sienna rocks and dirt rising up in mighty plateaus that dot the plain, and the robin's-egg gradient of the sky, deepening as it climbs away from the horizon. To underscore that God's paintbrush can't be replicated, Ethan has been dressed in a simple red shirt and blue neckerchief presenting a manufactured equivalent that pales in comparison.

To the people of the twentieth and twenty-first centuries, estranged from their hunter-gather roots, Westerns can provide a temporary reprieve from the domestication of life in cities and the spreading suburbs. The sky and soil's brilliance implied an invigorating fullness of experience; the sun shining into squinting eyes, winds whipping through billowing hair, the sharpened adrenaline of knowing that death can lurk around any corner in Apache country. The promise of this bracing freshness brought Ethan and pioneers like him toward the coast, but survival took a toll on their humanity. To hack it in an environment admired for its ferocious beauty, explorers had no choice but to revert back to their primal selves, a savagery that would bar Ethan from the very land he settled.

#B5C4E1
R181 G196 B225

#A28462
R162 G132 B98

#4D4129
R77 G65 B41

SOMETHING LIKE DÉJÀ VU

VERTIGO
ALFRED HITCHCOCK
1958

Deceptive intricacy is the modus operandi of Alfred Hitchcock, who elevated page-turners and potboilers into classics, with an unshowy finesse for camera placement and movement. When he did decide to indulge in a touch of conspicuous flash, however, the effect could be dizzying—as in this unimpeachable portrait of erotic obsession, when the controlling Scottie Ferguson first lays eyes on his fully transformed lover Judy. He notices that she's a dead ringer for his late ex Madeleine, and goes about making her over in the image of the woman he believes dead, from her hairdo to her clothing. He gets a load of Judy's new yet familiar look once the pair have adjourned to her suite at the Empire Hotel (an actual San Francisco stopover, now renamed after *Vertigo*), in a living room illuminated by the neon sign just outside her window.

A fittingly feverish atmosphere creeps in as score composer Bernard Herrmann's swooning strings ramp up and Judy steps out of her bedroom awash in a green haze of memory. A fog without origin holds the light emanating from the Empire sign, its hue first introduced via the expensive-looking green and purple material of Madeleine's dinner outfit (standing out against the burgundy walls of the dining room, red being Scottie's opposite coloration), and then again when Judy sports a plainer

green sweater dress alerting Scottie to the likeness. Here, the color splits the difference between the radioactive and the pure, Judy's ghostly aura reinforced by a near-transparency around her head in the top of the frame. Scottie's corrosive lust consumes him to the point that he can conflate the two women in the mist of his mind, sealed with the following kiss in which rear projection shows that he's mentally transported himself to the stables where he first smooched his Madeleine.

The film critic Roger Ebert boiled down the greenery's significance to a symbol of Scottie's fear of falling—both falling in love and falling off something tall; Hitchcock takes a more expansive approach, green coming to stand in for psychological subjectivity itself. The entire film lives inside that shade, captured in the day's state-of-the-art high-resolution VistaVision and transferred to peerlessly clear 70mm film. When deteriorating negatives required restoration decades later, preserving the absolute fidelity of that exact color was an imperative, with some sticklers accusing the team of taking liberties. Considering the plot at hand, it's all too appropriate that something essential might get lost in a project to recreate an unattainable past.

#53936D
R83 G147 B109

#3A442E
R58 G68 B46

THE INFINITE SANDBOX

LAWRENCE OF ARABIA
DAVID LEAN
1962

There's an argument to be made that this is why we started creating movies, that it was all building to this: from the immense sandy maelstrom of the Nefud desert, a figure wrapped in printer-paper white emerges. Because this man is T.E. Lawrence (portrayed by the preternaturally handsome Peter O'Toole), once the camera gets a little closer, we can see that he has what may very well be the bluest eyes in the history of the human species. Exhibition on extra-luminous 70mm film reels ensured that viewers were able to savor each hue in its finest form, his irises icy pools set against the arid dunes. Unmatched for sheer enormity, David Lean's epic earned its all-timer reputation primarily by virtue of its titanic scale, but there's more to behold in his account of the Arab Revolt during the First World War than size for its own sake.

Whiteness figures prominently in the exploits of Lawrence, both the color and the racial identity. The military officer devoted himself so wholly to the cause of pan-Arabian liberation from the empire he was supposed to be representing that his local liaisons took him in as one of their own, forcing him to reckon with the limits of this assimilation. He earns the respect of companion Sherif Ali ibn el Kharish by risking his own life to save one of their men, and after they call it a night, Sherif Ali replaces Lawrence's army uniform with his own culture's customary robes. In blinding, clean white, his costuming posits the conflicted identity of a Westerner struggling to fit in with his adopted nation. A treacherous trek through a dust storm leaves Lawrence's clothes and skin browned with dirt, his appearance externalizing the detachment he feels from his fellow officers at the British encampment he ultimately reaches. He feels he has less in common with them than with the humble Arabian soldiers in his small traveling party.

But Lawrence can, and does, wash himself back to spotlessness. Lean subverts the pat white savior narrative with more sober-minded cynicism than most present-day counterparts, concluding that, however meaningful, the robes were always just an outfit Lawrence could put on and take off as he pleased. After the revolution fizzles out and the British seize control, a defeated Lawrence saunters back to his home by the English Channel, whiling away his days until his death by motorcycle accident. He could support the Arab peoples, but he'd never be one of them. However he recolors himself, his eyes would always give himself away.

#7F899E
R127 G137 B158

#998D66
R153 G141 B102

#C1BDB7
R193 G189 B183

#9A8B75
R154 G139 B117

#683728
R104 G55 B40

2
UNBOUND
IMAGINATIONS

The rich colors used in Scorsese's *Taxi Driver* underscore the corruption of the city.

Although students of cinema invariably come to see art and commerce as mortal enemies stuck in an everlasting tug of war, they also share a symbiotic dependence that keeps both alive. Without the creative class, the pencil-pushers would have nothing to sell, and without the infrastructure of distribution and exhibition, filmmakers wouldn't be able to rake in any fruits from their labors. But the actions of C-suite execs, congresspeople, and scientists can also exert a more circuitous influence on films often read as a single artist's personal expression. Through the 1950s and 1960s, aftershocks from developments in the industry overworld of dealmakers and rule-setters reverberated outward and shook loose a tectonic expansion in style and content, with color the signpost marking how far the medium had come.

In 1948, the Supreme Court issued the Paramount Decree, barring studios from owning the movie theaters showing their releases, ruling that this vertical integration constituted a violation of antitrust laws. This freed up American movie houses to import foreign films, bringing intellectually curious viewers such building blocks of the cinematic canon as Ingmar Bergman's *The Seventh Seal* (1957) and Akira Kurosawa's *Seven Samurai* (1954). The growing appreciation for cinema as the high-minded "seventh art" led to the implementation of education courses at the university level, all of which contributed to a newly discerning class of viewers. They wanted serious movies from a serious art form, but Hollywood's maturation was stunted by the Hays Code. Enacted to tidy up a business seen as a cesspool of degeneracy in the 1930s, the draconian measures purged movies of sex, cuss words, drug use, violence—anything less than squeaky-clean upstanding morality. Fear of getting outpaced by the rest of the world, along with a need to give the people something the even-more-regulated TV could not, pressured the Motion Picture Association of America into replacing the Code with the rating system still displayed before each movie trailer.

By 1968, the gates had been thrown open, and a deluge of films using color in clever, unprecedented ways rushed in to fill the vacant space. Counterculture artefacts *Bonnie and Clyde* (Arthur Penn, 1967) and *Easy Rider* (Dennis Hopper, 1969) showed blood as it had never been seen before, picking up where splatter horror ungoverned by the Code had left off. The crop of upstart directors dubbed New Hollywood made hard-nosed realism their stock-in-trade over charmed showbiz confection, although films like *American Graffiti* (George Lucas, 1973) and *Taxi Driver* (Martin Scorsese, 1976) worked richer color back into their diagnoses of spiritual corruption. Far from the palm-tree-lined boulevards of California, hippie-nerds in the Astralvision collective at the University of Illinois in Chicago sent video art into the stratosphere with Electronic Visualization Events, spaced-out live performances of video synthesizer feedback played like an instrument with shifting colors as its notes.

During this time, the most exploratory reinventions of color came to the States from overseas. Bergman and Kurosawa both gave in after holding fast to black and white for longer than most, unable to resist the temptation of adding another dimension to the authorial trademarks they'd spent decades honing. European young guns Jacques Demy and Rainer Werner Fassbinder built a bridge to America with their salutes to the multicolor magnificence of yesteryear's Hollywood genres. Kodak's pride-and-joy film stock Eastmancolor supplanted Technicolor with a lower price point and a less involved development process, a boon in particular to the industries of Africa (as seen in *Touki Bouki*, page 72) and India (as seen in *Bobby*, page 76). The end of Technicolor spelled the end of an ebullient escapist Hollywood, its colors never again so brilliant. But any lost visual latitude was more than made up for by breadth of concept, as a band of iconoclasts around the globe dynamited traditional assumptions about what cinema could be and do.

Cinema is unique among the major art forms in its often-prohibitive price tag. Painters, sculptors, and musicians have made do with whatever resources they've had at hand, but a film cannot be made without a camera and, in the medium's earliest days, stock onto which that camera could record. This great, sudden market demand in the late nineteenth century precipitated the meteoric rise of the Eastman Kodak Company, the motor that drove Hollywood's dream factory. Although Kodak began in still photography, its products enabled Thomas Edison to contrive moving pictures in the first place, and they were established as the industry standard once the Tinseltown studio system took shape in California.

Kodak introduced the groundbreaking color stock Kodachrome in 1935—three years after founder George Eastman took his own life at 77, declaring "my work is done, why wait?"—and used it initially on stills and non-commercial projects shot with smaller 16mm cameras. Their product line grew quickly in variety and popularity, most notably with the advent of the handheld Super 8 camera and Eastmancolor, a proprietary film processing technology that would soon overtake the beloved yet labor-intensive Technicolor. Several of the selected works in this section (*Cries and Whispers*, *2001: A Space Odyssey*, *The Umbrellas of Cherbourg*) gained their

brilliant luster courtesy of Kodak's equipment, the brightness and clarity coming to stand as synonymous with the company's name. For a present-day viewer looking back on a classic, the warmth and softness identified with "old" movies is a function of Kodak's trademarked palette—nostalgia, packaged and shipped by the ton.

Kodak attempted to hold onto its monopoly in the United States for as long as it could; it took a 1954 court order to force the company to allow other photo processing labs to work on Kodachrome film. Kodak was primed for a competitor and got one by way of Japan, where the Fujifilm corporation had earned a deep foothold by merit of their low prices and vivid color exposures. Confident that they'd never lose the American dollar, executives at Kodak made a fatal error in passing up a chance to be an official sponsor of the 1984 Los Angeles Olympics, an opportunity Fujifilm seized as a way into America. They opened a plant in the United States four years later, and unveiled their crown jewel Velvia as a rival to Kodachrome. (The 1998 Robin Williams picture *What Dreams May Come*, directed by Vincent Ward, bears the distinction of being one of the few features shot on Velvia, its searing azures intended to imitate both living paintings and the kingdom of heaven.)

KODAK AND FUJIFILM

A Fujifilm billboard on the Sunset Strip in Los Angeles in 1984, when they were an official sponsor of the Los Angeles Olympics.

The ongoing feud between the two companies, complete with impotent litigation and desperate internal restructuring, waned as they both entered a period of decline. The shift to digital cinematography would be kind to neither, driving Kodak to bankruptcy in 2012 and Fujifilm to cease production of stock in 2013. Kodak tried to sell the public on the Ektra, a smartphone that would reproduce their house coloration, to no avail. Kodachrome was discontinued in phases through the 2000s, until only one laboratory in smalltown Kansas bothered to continue developing it, calling it quits in 2011. Fujifilm has thrived by diversifying, leaving the entertainment industry behind for biotech. While Kodak has attempted to follow suit, getting in the pharmaceutical chemical game during the Covid-19 pandemic, they've also taken care to maintain their connection to and support of the movie world.

Each year, some of the most artistically adventurous releases take on an added air of prestige by shooting on still-manufactured Kodak stock as opposed to a digital video drive; the likes of Last Night in Soho (Edgar Wright), The French Dispatch (Wes Anderson), and Steven Spielberg's West Side Story remake—all from 2021—emulate the past and its bygone aesthetics through the visible grain and lived-in colors of the filmstrip. In the modern film economy, financial constraints and lack of technical know-how have made this method more of a novelty, but it will persist as long as the love of film itself. For those keyed in to history, Kodak's film contains the essence of cinema, as a delicate craft powered by human ingenuity.

A FRENCH LOVE LETTER

THE UMBRELLAS OF CHERBOURG
JACQUES DEMY 1964

Jacques Demy's delightful, bittersweet French New Wave staple isn't just the most effervescent screen musical of the 1960s, but an impassioned defence of the genre itself. The director was enraptured with the three-ring circuses of Old Hollywood music men Vincente Minnelli and Stanley Donen at toe-tapper-happy studio MGM, and so for his first foray into their domain, he set out to encapsulate everything he loved about those films. (A few years later, he'd land the real big fish and cast Gene Kelly in the similarly tuneful *The Young Girls of Rochefort*.) Every line of dialogue takes the form of conversational singsong, an acquired taste joked about in the first scene through a mechanic's whining over "all the singing" in opera. But Demy's bedrock of adoring allusion is most apparent in his fondness for that Hollywood feeling, the ability to draw the ecstatic out from the unremarkable—a remembrance of a fantasy, sentimentalized twice over by the time it gets to us.

As is musical tradition, the ardor between dashing grease monkey Guy and umbrella boutique shopgirl Geneviève perks up the mundanity of the Normandy port town where they catch each other's eyes. Costume designer Jacqueline Moreau, set designer Bernard Evein, and cinematographer Jean Rabier regularly synced their work to confirm that they were all using the same bank of burnished color options. The chic mademoiselles loitering in Cherbourg's main plaza match their primary-colored couture to their nails, jewellery, or hair. They sometimes blend into the scene-stealing wallpaper, which wraps the charming French soundstages in *macaron* tones of pink or green. The film's shattering coda, which reunites the ill-fated pair years after their lives take a diverging fork, falls on a night with its color erased by the blanch of snow.

The semi-downer ending sends our romantic leads apart into the lives they've learned to appreciate, its conflicted poignancy out of joint with the musical's usual happily-ever-after ending. The genre's joyous rush of escape is turned on its head, now a wistful reverie about the marriage they've missed the chance to make real. But the last thing Demy wanted was to get mired in the dour, and he decorated his film to sustain the musical's zest even as he undercut it. He subscribes to the old chestnut about parting being such sweet sorrow, to the extent that we can't have one without the other. A rose-tinted girlhood ends in woe; a random, frigid meet-up can thaw into a qualified contentment.

 #C2798D
R194 G121 B141

 #708764
R112 G135 B100

 #A7A38C
R167 G163 B140

#5A7A8D
R90 G122 B141

#A76990
R167 G105 B144

#4B426F
R75 G66 B111

#AA6844
R170 G104 B68

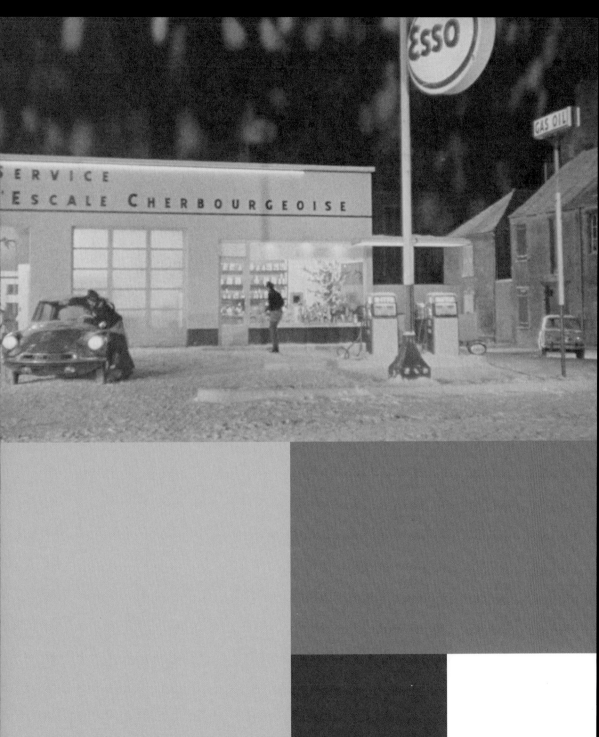

#ADAA9E
R0173 G170 B158

#995C54
R153 G92 B84

#333951
R51 G57 B81

HOSTILE ATMOSPHERE

RED DESERT
MICHELANGELO ANTONIONI 1964

"Why should I work when the sun is out?" Italy's Michelangelo Antonioni asked himself in a 1964 interview with *The New York Times*. "I would be like a painter who found that half of his canvas already was sky blue. I prefer to work on location in real surroundings, but if a façade should be a different colour for the mood of a scene, I paint it the way I want it." This was his policy going in to his first color feature, *Red Desert*, its judiciously assembled palette refining his considerations of ennui, alienation, and other heavy-duty pet topics of the Euro arthouse. On afternoons so clogged with cloud cover that the air seems to sit on the ground, he erected colossal monuments to man's machinery of self-destruction in a tundra of sleet-tone gray with only the most foreboding, unseemly color poking through.

Giuliana, played by Monica Vitti, walks around the dilapidated Technicolor wasteland of Ravenna looking for signs of life, finding only rusty siloes or glass bottles of indeterminate use. Their brown and green may break up the homogeneity of this landscape, but they also exemplify how the more vivid elements of Antonioni's *mise en scène* don't signify the things they usually do in contrast to gray—purity, resilience, saplings rising through cracks in cement, etc. Every time Giuliana thinks she's found something real, it slips through her grasp. She strikes up a tentative courtship with a colleague of her inattentive husband, their flicker of attraction channeled into the red walls of a shack where they spend an amorous day with another couple. As the day goes on, these boards will be broken and used for kindling, Giuliana's last ember of spirit burning away with them.

Antonioni coaxes harshness from beauty and vice versa, acknowledging that devastation can be spectacular and that loveliness is fleeting if it's not false. Under the impression her young son has come down with polio and joined her in sadness, Giuliana regales him with a fable about a girl living in a cove, shot on the pink sands of the Spiaggia Rosa on the island of Budelli. She's trying to commiserate, but once her son drops the act and shows her he was just playing a game, she's even more despondent than before. Bringing him past a chemical plant, the plumes of yellow smoke whisper that they and the hazards they represent cannot be evaded, only avoided, like the birds that Giuliana notes have learned to fly away from the belching gas. Caught between toxic colors and the featureless tracts of gray they leave denuded, she's at the mercy of an environment less habitable by the day.

#6B7477
R107 G116 B119

#66656B
R102 G101 B107

#E2C5B4
R226 G197 B180

#652E19
R101 G46 B25

#261D15
R38 G29 B21

#908D98
R144 G141 B152

#B99E59
R185 G158 B89

KILLER STYLES

COLOR ME BLOOD RED
HERSCHELL GORDON LEWIS 1965

Among horror aficionados, recipes for fake blood vary, with experts individually devising their own trade-secret formula through years of trial and error. For the most part, it comes down to a calibrated mixture of corn syrup (Karo brand preferred by the pros), water thinning to the desired viscosity, and the all-important dye to get that fresh-out-of-the-vein look. In the days of yore, the Hays Code's censorship minimized the carnage that could be shown on screen, and black and white filming meant that blood need only be dark. Because its natural tone photographed as a dull gray on camera, directors like Alfred Hitchcock sometimes substituted chocolate syrup, the special ingredient in the shower slaughter from *Psycho* (1960). With the arrival of color and the relaxing of puritanical standards, a slew of questions complicated the making of fake blood. How red is too red? Or not red enough? Should the goal be medical accuracy, or theatrical effect?

Enter Herschell Gordon Lewis, the Godfather of Gore and progenitor of what's now affectionately known as splatter cinema. In ramshackle B-movies exempt from the Hays Code dictates, he uncorked geysers of viscera in Day-Glo shades bordering on the luminescent. Unconcerned with realism,

his films popularized a gaudy palette that would inform the next few decades of low-rent horror flicks, in which that obvious ersatz quality made all the difference between "disturbing" and "disturbing, but in a fun way." *Color Me Blood Red* completed an informal Blood Trilogy setting the pace for its mini-genre, the third instalment enriched by an accented mindfulness about its grisly style. In the film, a painter grows fixated on procuring just the right shade of red to make his canvasses stand out from the herd, and resorts to a homicidal spree upon realizing that only human blood will do the trick.

As the bodies pile up, gore and inspiration commingle in the maniac's psyche until they're inseparable from one another. In his puckish treatment of the hipster-beatnik demi-monde, particularly the beret-wearing critic who tells our murder-happy artist that "your use of colour is not – let us be generous – not developed," Lewis thumbs his nose at anyone who'd look down on him as a purveyor of trash. (Or rather, anyone who thought of "trash" as a pejorative.) His every brushstroke was as purposeful and labored over as his on-screen alter ego's—irrefutable evidence that there's a skill to fine-tuning the lurid. Flesh wounds would never be the same again.

#792E1E
R121 G46 B30

#888373
R136 G131 B115

#D8C2B5
R216 G194 B181

#792E1E
R121 G46 B30

#70707D
R112 G112 B125

#D8C2B5
R216 G194 B181

PSYCHEDELIC VORTEXES

2001: A SPACE ODYSSEY
STANLEY KUBRICK 1968

Experimental film has existed as long as film itself, but to permeate the mainstream, the avant-garde would require a giant of no less than Stanley Kubrick's stature. By 1968, he'd amassed enough industry clout to earn MGM's confidence (and money) for an unorthodox adaptation of a short story by sci-fi titan Arthur C. Clarke, in which looser conceptual threads connect his ideas. The open-mindedness of the counterculture era made a box-office hit out of a head trip steeped in abstraction, whisking the viewer from a prehistoric cradle of life to the deepest reaches of outer space to the ends of the galaxy. And there, Dr David Bowman, the last remaining survivor aboard the *Discovery* after the sentient computer HAL snuffs out the puny homo sapiens threatening its existence, tumbles into a vortex and leaves all sense behind.

The technically and creatively pioneering sequence that follows, known either as the "Star Gate" or the "Jupiter and Beyond the Infinite" sequence, jettisons Bowman at light speed into a hyperstream of pure color and energy. Kubrick and special effects supervisor Douglas Trumbull were the first to smuggle psychedelia into the multiplex, sucking their audience into a lava-lamp dimension that bleeds from a full electric rainbow through its individual parts, reds and yellows giving way to greens and indigos. Rather than splotches fading in and out, however, the kinetic lights simulate the camera's movement between two flat planes stretching into eternity, an illusion achieved through a complex process known as slit-scan photography. Trumbull's crew mounted a long-exposure camera on a track facing a black sheet with a thin slit, behind which an image could be run for a stretching, distorting effect while the lens moves forward. Each exposure captured this way took about a minute, and each frame of film consisted of two exposures, demanding an inordinate amount of time and effort for a brief yet indelible spectacle.

What it was all supposed to mean was lost on plenty of ticket-buyers at the time of release, and continues to spur heated debate among scholars and stoners alike today. But wrestling the text into orderly answers goes against the spirit of the sensory avalanche Kubrick and his collaborators designed. It washes over a person, overwhelming them on a visceral level with the blizzard of Lite-Brite lasers. The film's most revolutionary moments dared to wonder whether we needed to comprehend these perception-melting passages to understand them.

 #000000
R0 G0 B0

 #ba5451
R186 G84 B81

 #54723e
R84 G114 B62

 #754f88
R117 G79 B136

A WOMB IN RED

CRIES AND WHISPERS
INGMAR BERGMAN 1972

The corpus of Sweden's foremost filmmaking grandmaster Ingmar Bergman is so bonded to the innermost stuff of the self—anguish, fury, absolution—that it's no wonder the idea for his *Cries and Whispers* came to him in a dream. In the press, he got a lot of mileage out of the anecdote that he was visited in sleep by a vision of four women in white gowns, whispering to one another within a room of fathoms-deep red. He molded this bolt of inspiration into a chamber drama about a dying girl tended to by her spiteful sisters and a more dutiful housemaid, though the most important input from his slumbering neurons was the background that would come to command the film.

Bergman laid ruddy crimsons all over his rhapsody on mortality, funneling the Freudian mess death leaves behind into the color he thought of as "the interior of the soul." The ailing lead, Agnes, wastes away from uterine cancer in the stony confines of the Taxinge-Näsby Castle, her bedroom festooned with wallpaper and curtains that make the space look like a womb or a failing organ. Cinematographer Sven Nykvist netted an Oscar for his diligent matching of the reds—the most sensitive register for the Eastmancolor stock to pick up, necessitating a "huge amount" of screen tests to pre-empt over- or underexposure—to the skin tones,

make-up, and dresses of the actresses, all shot under natural light streaming in through the windows. The beatific, funereal calm indoors clashes with the more unrestful manifestations of red, such as the blood haemorrhaging after one sister lacerates herself with a shard of glass in a flashback to drive away her husband. We're all made out of red, a notion Bergman carries to the cinematic by dividing scenes with a fade to red instead of black. Cut the film, and it bleeds.

The red outlines the limits of the dysfunctional yet intimate familial status quo the sisters can't bear to relinquish, and the outlying shots show their anxiety about leaving it. One of the few black frames falls within the aforementioned flashback, in a close-up of the doleful Karin just as the crystal glass she will use to self-harm breaks for no reason. Away from her sisters, under the hawklike gaze of her humorless spouse, she's at her darkest and the colors tell us so. But, however acute the injuries those closest to us can inflict, they're still all we've got. The Edenic final scene visits a fonder stop on memory lane, as the girls and the maid share a ride on a swing as equals, the golden streaks of magic hour all around them. When it feels like the red of long-simmering resentment is filling one's lungs, all we need do is go and get some fresh air.

#5F301F
R95 G48 B31

#BFCDCE
R191 G205 B206

#6F6C47
R111 G108 B71

#4E3723
R78 G55 B35

#C8CECD
R200 G206 B205

DREAMS OF SENEGAL

Senegalese filmmaker Djibril Diop Mambéty thought of himself as precisely that. In the years after the West African nation gained independence in 1960, an exodus of youths took off for Paris, a bastion of development offering greater opportunity for social mobility relative to the provincial capital city Dakar. Mambéty repudiated this migration and stayed put in his home, opting instead to teach himself the trade (taking pointers from the form-warping mavericks of the French New Wave) and map the Senegal they'd all left behind. Through his two features and handful of shorts prior to his passing too soon at fifty-three, he turned his back to Europe in politics and style, declining their artistic methodologies along with the invitation to join a white society.

Made at the age of twenty-eight with a rumored budget of US$30,000 (a meagre US$194,000 in today's money), his feature debut *Touki Bouki* ("The Journey of the Hyena") finds post-colonial Africa pulled in opposite directions, a friction indicated by the hodgepodge attitude toward editing, narrative structure, and color. While the techs at the Martin Scorsese-fronted World Cinema Project worked wonders on the intact prints of this long-scarce film, their 2008 restoration couldn't smooth out all the inconsistencies. The good news is that viewers can still see the richness of the saturation, and how it changes as the villages on the

outskirts give way to the density of Dakar. The opening shot sits transfixed on a pair of cowherds nudging along their livestock, the cattle unaware that they're being ushered into a slaughterhouse for disembowelment. The commentary on how the rise of industry has affected tribespeople is as subtle as a saw to the neck, yet Mambéty also drives home his outrage in a less overt manner by setting the savannah's earthy tones against the blood and steel of the abattoir.

Once the elliptical story latches on to Mory and Anta, young lovers arranging to skip town and engineer a second act in France, the colors point to the commercialism that's taken a bite out of Senegal. The organically dyed, loose-fitting boubous worn by rural women are replaced by hipper 1970s clothes in up-to-date tones, such as the grays and lavenders of the mass-produced Bonnie and Clyde cosplay donned by Mory and Anta during a series of petty thefts to fund their boat tickets. One of their heists garners a car, which cues up an unforgettable demonstration of revolt: Mory stands triumphantly in the passenger seat and strips naked as he sings a song from the West African oral troubadours called griots. The star-spangled paint job on their ride looks flimsy and disposable next to the infinite ground and the sky, now bluer than it was before. Senegal will exist forever, long after the bright, cheap imports have expired.

#CA4E34
R202 G78 B52

#776C5B
R119 G108 B91

#AC8C64
R172 G140 B100

#EADCE9
R234 G220 B233

#DBE9F3
R219 G233 B243

#E0C8AD
R224 G200 B173

#A3673F
R163 G103 B63

#C1D9D0
R193 G217 B208

#949D87
R148 G157 B135

#96655E
R150 G101 B94

HOORAY FOR BOLLYWOOD

BOBBY
RAJ KAPOOR
1973

Hollywood may have the edge in terms of cashflow, but India's film industry dwarfs its American counterpart on annual tickets sold and number of releases. Nearly two thousand new titles per year foster a hardcore movie madness in this massive market, where the ritual of cinema-going has an amplified sense of ceremony to it. Masala films—blockbusting mash-ups of action, romance, humor, and drama, as opposed to India's "parallel cinema" of social realism—exalt in their own glorious muchness, jampacking as many musical numbers, fights, and assorted diversions as the three-hour run times can hold. The more-is-more aesthetic is a cornerstone of Bollywood, the Hindi-language production hub in Mumbai that makes up the largest chunk of the Indian mainstream.

Raj Kapoor's masala picture par excellence *Bobby* became India's highest grosser of 1973 (and one of the country's all-time top earners, adjusting for inflation) by joining the default maximalist mode with a fledgling teen culture perfectly suited to its big, unwieldy feelings and popping palette. Hormones run amok as the well-heeled Raja sets his sights on the tantalizing Bobby, daughter to a penniless Christian farmer from the Goa region, and their instantaneous puppy love harmonizes with the colors that intensify every minute

they share. Raja goes to ask Bobby's father for her hand at a raucous party already in full swing, with strings of lights in red, yellow, blue, and green providing a link to the rest of the decor. Stained glass in red and green and a house's façade painted in light blue follow the jolly inauthenticity native to the musical, and the backdrop painted for sunset tells the tale: this is the vibrant, invented India that American executives were looking for from Renoir's underplayed *The River*.

If anything, Kapoor reshaped Indian fashions, which adapted to follow his film's example. Sixteen-year-old star Dimple Kapadia was christened a style icon among legions of teenyboppers for her envelope-pushing sartorial sense; the flamboyant dyes once coveted by colonizers were transferred from full-body saris and other old-world garb to miniskirts and crop tops all the rage in Europe. She's wrapped tightly in red fabric coordinated with a headpiece when Raja sidles up to her, his Tiffany-blue leisure suit making them a matching pair. They may be mooning over each other as only those caught up in foolhardy first love can, but with their surroundings and wardrobe as jubilant as their hearts, who wouldn't believe that they'll last forever?

#E09F8F
R224 G159 B143

#CB3F81
R203 G63 B129

#9BC4A3
R155 G196 B163

DEATH IS A STALKER

DON'T LOOK NOW
NICOLAS ROEG
1973

Nicolas Roeg's pillar of British horror, *Don't Look Now*, starts at the unthinkable. In a discombobulating flurry of cross-cutting, he shows historian John Baxter examining a photo slide of the Italian church he'll soon restore as pint-sized daughter Christine frolics and drowns in the back garden of their English country manor. The stuttering edits create implicit associations that'll recur as the film unfurls: John's son bicycles over a windowpane as John knocks over a drinking glass inside, tagging broken shards as an important motif, and Christine's red jacket corresponds to a similarly hooded figure John spots in the photo. The spill from the glass expands onto the slide and merges with the unseen person's red raincoat, spreading into the rest of the frame like a virus. Roeg's not just informing us that red will be the cardinal color, he's showing us how it moves—through membranes, past limits, around rationality.

As John and his wife Laura take to Venice for his job, losing themselves in the waterways of a foreign city also seems to help with the grieving process. But the image of his daughter's red jacket, branded into John's brain after he lifts her from her watery grave, won't leave him alone. On top of seeing it every time he closes his eyes, red accents follow him wherever he goes, hiding in jewelry, bunting, architectural curlicues. While most of these don't register for him, he does catch sight of another diminutive red-jacket-wearer, who then scampers away and periodically skulks around the periphery of his awareness. He thinks he's seen Christine, convinced by the words of a blind seer that he and his wife meet at a restaurant earlier that day. A chase through the dank maze of Venice (its mildewy blacks and browns directing sightlines to the scraps of red) at the film's climax will unmask the horrifying truth to him.

John realizes too late that his baffling visions were actually omens of his own death, his linear concept of time coming undone along with Roeg's. Mementos and premonitions intermingle around the lattice of vaporetto paths, itself an analogue for the pond that claimed Christine's life. As the audience adjusts to these off-putting conditions, reds can be a signpost, although they lead us astray as often as they show us the way. Hats, flowers, or sheets on drying lines portend a threat long before we realize where or what it is, their feeling of discomfort worming its way in and gnawing at the back of the head. That a viewer spends the rest of their day more keenly, warily observant of the various reds in their own life, is Roeg's coup de grace.

● #90352B
R144 G53 B43

● #7B9298
R123 G146 B152

● #BD8B71
R189 G139 B113

#2E2C21
R46 G44 B33

#9B372F
R155 G55 B47

#5C6951
R92 G105 B81

#50554F
R80 G85 B79

#562712
R86 G39 B18

#221F00
R34 G31 B00

THE REST THAT HEAVEN ALLOWED

ALI: FEAR EATS THE SOUL
RAINER WERNER FASSBINDER 1974

A lonesome older woman and a younger man exuding undiluted testosterone fall for one another, crossing dividing lines of class and dismaying their respective social circles. If that sounds familiar, it should—West Germany's pre-eminent filmmaker Rainer Werner Fassbinder idolized Douglas Sirk, and purloined the plot of *All That Heaven Allows* (see page 38) for an impossible romance of his own. (One character kicks in a TV during an angry outburst, Fassbinder's reference to Sirk's symbol of homebound solitude.) But his tribute is a beast all of its own, and not just in the rejigging of the central couple to add the wrinkle of race through the Moroccan-born Ali. While holding onto the bones of its predecessor's driving conflict and bruised romanticism, he gave its formal framework a top-to-bottom makeover.

Fassbinder's recapitulation goes to tenser, terser places, situated not in pastoral blue-blood America but in the shadow of the Nazi regime and the terrorist attacks at the 1972 Olympics, both of which engendered a culture of normalized discrimination against Muslims. The compositions are wide and sparse, the dialogue is clipped and infrequent, and Sirk's saturation has been toned way down. Ali and Emmi come together in a Munich of cost-effective apartment block stairwells and alleys winding between them,

the improbable pair bringing color to the melange of gray and tan. Fassbinder opts for a more consistent symbolism than Sirk's holistic richness, however, designating red and yellow as the ones to watch for.

Emmi and Ali meet cutely during a rainstorm, moved to slow dance as the jukebox plays what they'll come to savor as "their song" under lights as red as their pumping blood. Yellow tiptoes into the film as their differences put a strain on their relationship, most blatant in a shot stranding them in a snare of daffodil-colored chairs, distanced from everyone they used to know. Ali's insecurities and Emmi's need to be liked by her erstwhile Third Reich gal-pals throw a wrench into their simple marriage, but of course they make up as melodrama law rules they must. She circles back to the same bar in the hopes that dancing to the same song will spark the same emotions, and the shot of her arrival lays out their discord: while Ali sits with his bohemian-ish friends (their of-the-time outfits in contrast with his gray suit of stoicism) at a red table in the foreground, Emmi appears in the doorway and steps out of the yellow light backing her. Ali's perforated ulcer puts a tragic expiration date on their union, but cradling one another under the red lights as personal to them as the song they share is enough for the time being.

#688565
R104 G133 B101

#494534
R73 G69 B52

#D8BC7B
R216 G188 B123

#7EB8B1
R126 G184 B177

#632D16
R99 G45 B22

#2F2100
R47 G33 B0

#2F2100
R47 G33 B0

#7B4939
R123 G73 B57

#445A69
R68 G90 B105

A WOMAN'S WORK

JEANNE DIELMAN ... CHANTAL AKERMAN 1975

Jeanne Dielman wakes up. She shines her son's shoes before he leaves for the day. She folds laundry. She eats the most pathetic sandwich in cinema history. She puts on potatoes to boil for dinner. She ministers to one of the men who stop by during the day to pay her for sex. Her son returns, and she eats next to him, mostly in silence. She listens to a little music. She goes to sleep. Although she occasionally ventures out of the house to run errands or morosely sip a coffee in a neighborhood café, this routine—begun while married to the late husband whose ring she still wears, kept up for the sake of the son who's taken his place—is her prison, and the house is her cell.

Chantal Akerman's quintessential feminist film (full title *Jeanne Dielman, 23, quai du commerce, 1080 Bruxelles*) places the viewer inside the crushing tedium that quietly desperate housewife Jeanne lives with every day, just as it comes to overpower her. In lengthy, unmoving shots, she performs household chores in real time, kneading meatloaf for minutes upon minutes while we're helpless to watch her go through her rote motions. The stifling boredom beats down on her from all directions in the deadness of her Brussels flat's spartan decor, her lack of stimulation reflected in the milquetoast color scheme. She's surrounded by products of metal and cut-rate plastic, post-war purchases in cheery synthetics dulled over the years, just like her. The lack of living things is most pronounced in the den, where a motel-lobby-quality painting of a park scene in wilted greens makes nature itself look worn out and tired.

Jeanne spends her most forlorn hours at the kitchen table, locked in both the frame and her domestic role. She's enveloped by mildness, the tiles behind her in a yellow so blah that they're nearly tan, almost blending in with the dish rack and bowl to the left. The bottle of soap and scrubbing brush hanging on the wall also share a single shade, pointing out the stultifying lack of variety in Jeanne's day-to-day. In the possessions meant to last—her curtains, her housecoat, her coffee pot—she adds a smidgen of flair with tartans or other patterns, but Akerman's office-complex lighting saps the energy from the green, blue, and red. There's no room to breathe, and she'll take rash measures to break through the walls she can feel closing in on her. For women consigned to a life of servitude by a patriarchal society, however, freeing yourself isn't so clear-cut. Jeanne bucks the expected, but once she does, she can only sit back down at the same tomblike kitchen, her world no brighter.

 #757765 R117 G119 B101

 #5B503C R91 G80 B60

 #3C4042 R60 G64 B66

 #72423A R114 G66 B58

THREE-IN-ONE

GOD TOLD ME TO
LARRY COHEN
1976

Maestro of the peculiar Larry Cohen starts *God Told Me To* as a horror film, segues into a police procedural, and finishes with sci-fi. The supremely unsettling first act catalogues a string of ostensibly random acts of violence around Manhattan, from a sniper opening fire on unsuspecting civilians to an abrupt, out-of-nowhere supermarket stabbing. They're all united by the given rationale of the title, a pattern that sounds alarm bells for Peter Nicholas, the devoutly Catholic detective on the case. His dogged sleuthing fills out the middle of the film, and brings him into contact with a quasi-religious cult led by a prophet (possibly of the false variety, though that's left up to us) who claims to be descended from aliens and has a gender-ambiguous genital orifice just below the ribs. This unclassifiable potpourri of genres was business as usual for Cohen, a boundary-breaker managing his collaged influences through color.

Peter wends his way through the hardscrabble New York of the 1970s, a culturally fertile time and place that still looms large in the public's nostalgic memory due to the myth-making of Cohen and his contemporaries. He saw the allure in this crime-ridden jungle of garbage, and Peter's gumshoe activities flaunt the buzzy urban setting that only a city-slicker could love. The coloration is unaccented yet alive, the bands of sky and gray-brown high-rises as dramatic as Rothko's striated paintings. But as Cohen eases his creative purview toward horror, he drops in blots of red and green with no place in the normal city palette, seen in Peter's harrowing run-in with the cult leader's unhinged mother that culminates in her death. (In a film interrogating the piety of Christianity, the twisting of the old Yuletide color scheme into a harbinger of danger can't be coincidental.)

Cohen's slippery screenplay changes shape again once Peter gets his non-man, tracking the self-fashioned messiah to his lair in a boiler room. The inferno-adjacent locale may have us thinking of hell, but Cohen overlooks red or orange for a yellow not of this world, a sour-lemon exposure at a high contrast suggesting the spotlight of a UFO about to abduct. By marking its changes through visual signposts, the film slides into drive-in sci-fi territory without running the risk of disjointedness—rather than being all over the place, it slithers from one place to the next. By the final shot, Peter has been indoctrinated, and we're left feeling as disorientated as he did starting out.

#eed855
R238 G216 B85

#644e30
R100 G78 B48

#332800
R51 G40 B00

#71867E
R113 G134 B126

#6A695E
R106 G105 B94

#504743
R80 G71 B67

THE DANSE MACABRE

SUSPIRIA
DARIO ARGENTO
1977

Dario Argento's most widely seen fever dream of horror is blanketed in death, the most significant of which happens off screen. In the travails of Suzy Bannion, an American ballerina unaware that her instructors at a rigorous German dance academy happen to be witches, the Italian director sounded out an operatic funeral dirge for the waning Technicolor. His film would be among the last produced using the technology, cooked up at the only functional facility left in Rome, and he made sure to send it out with a bang. Trading the usual emulsion-based processing for the specialty "imbibition" that electrified *Gone with the Wind* (1939) with more stable dyes, he was able to reach new heights of the nightmarish. The rehearsal halls and well-appointed lounges mutate into a funhouse from which Suzy has no hope of escape.

Although Argento was after the same paint-like quality originated by Herschell Gordon Lewis for all the bloodshed, he gets more varied use out of a brighter red in keeping with the surreal ambience. A fluorescent cousin of magenta pops up the exterior of the Tanz Dance Akademie, a few indoor accent walls, stained-glass panels in the windows, and the curtains lining the corridors leading to a forbidden sanctum. Unexplained blue, green, and yellow lights slink in from places they have no business being, removing Suzy from any footing in reality that might make her feel safe. While he still had the time, Argento wanted to push Technicolor to within an inch of its life. "We were trying to reproduce the colour of Walt Disney's *Snow White*," he said of his reasoning. "It has been said from the beginning that Technicolor lacked subdued shades, [and] was without nuances – like cut-out cartoons."

Argento flouted horror convention by operating from the premise that being able to see could be far more frightening than the unknown. His command of light and color were so surgical that, when remaking the film in 2018, director Luca Guadagnino knew better than to try and outdo his predecessor. He went as far as he could in the other direction, slathering on muted browns and ashen grays for a pervasive gloom, which only served to reaffirm the luminosity of the original. Argento took his inimitable palette from the recesses of the subconscious, plunging his audience into a night terror that lingers long after the end credits wake us up.

#6583B9
R101 G131 B185

#8A3733
R138 G55 B51

#3A1A04
R58 G26 B4

#EDDC55
R237 G220 B85

#93B95A
R147 G185 B90

#3E5794
R62 G87 B148

#C84143
R200 G65 B67

WAR IS HELL

RAN
AKIRA
KUROSAWA
1985

After putting Japanese cinema on the map, mid-century great Akira Kurosawa found himself on its fringes as he entered his career's latter phase, made to seek funding and co-producers elsewhere. This did nothing to diminish his monomaniacal need for perfection, and the jump to color film only gave him more to pore over. With his final samurai epic *Ran*, he requisitioned the equivalent of US$11 million in French money for the most expensive production Japan had ever seen, bringing upward of a thousand extras and two hundred horses into the grassy knolls of Mount Aso, Japan's largest active volcano. Upon this awesome turf, from its moors of green to its sulfurous plains of black, Kurosawa made color look as godly as the clash-of-the-titans story it kept in order.

The power struggle between feudal warlords follows the broad contours of *King Lear*'s plot: an ageing ruler splits his fiefdom up between his three adult children, and a free-for-all breaks out as they jockey for the throne. The ensuing war ensnares three armies and a handful of self-interested operators playing all sides against the middle, a hectic scrum (*ran* is Japanese for "chaos") cohering through color. Each son and their battalions—eldest Taro in yellow, middle Jiro in red, and youngest Saburo in blue—tell friend from foe in the bedlam of arrows

and gunfire by the color of the uniforms that took designer Emi Wada to the Oscar stage. The movements and formations of these three primary colors clue us in to their standing with father Hidetora, clad in white (the neutral base color that breaks up into yellow, red, and blue) with red accents (for the innocent blood tarnishing his merciless legacy). After Jiro and Taro's united forces raze one of the three castles to be bequeathed, a dazed Hidetora staggers out and the armies part before him like the Red Sea, the path formed by yellow and red indicative of the respect his sons have, even in betrayal.

More than just handy, Kurosawa saw color as a self-evident source of beauty. He was besotted with the post-Impressionist elan of Van Gogh, who'd appear in Kurosawa's following film *Dreams* (1990) in a cameo by Martin Scorsese. *Ran*'s indispensable location shooting met these ambitions with a depth of field that went on for miles, the mountains in the background fading to lighter and lighter blues as they get further away. With a jaw-dropping foundation on which to arrange his gargantuan wide shots, Kurosawa turned this squabble among siblings into a bombastic brawl between jealous demigods grappling for immortality—an appropriate air of the almighty for a film that plays like a thunderbolt thrown from cinema's Olympus.

#669894
R102 G152 B148

#C19378
R193 G147 B120

#C7AC4F
R199 G172 B79

#495B33
R73 G91 B51

#C7A73F
R199 G167 B63

#39433B
R57 G67 B59

#7C3127
R124 G49 B39

#6888AD
R104 G136 B173

#649F69
R100 G159 B105

#CA6856
R202 G104 B86

3
MAKING A STATEMENT

Laura Dern stars in David Lynch's *Inland Empire*.

The roll-out of Eastmancolor meant that just about anyone making a feature film at the professional level could afford to shoot in color. The next step would be opening up access to the regular Joes and Janes who wanted no more than to preserve the excitement of their young 'uns on Christmas morning. The Super 8 camera (named for its 8mm film stock, major motion pictures being shot on 35mm or 65mm) brought with it the first wave of home movies, but there were drawbacks: the film's development could be bungled and processing time put a long delay on the enjoyment, not to mention the irksome cost of one-use-only reels. The solution came with the spread of amateur-ready digital videotape through the 1980s and 1990s, which recorded light and color as a pattern of electrical charges on a magnetized strip. (Since the 1970s, cameras compatible with larger tape-head gauges had been around productions official enough for a budget but not released in cinemas.) MiniDV cassette tapes were inexpensive, could be overwritten and were ready for playback as soon as you hit the red recording button.

The one hitch was that the footage captured by camcorders bore little resemblance to cinema as anyone knew it at the time. Motion jittered and lagged, lights were disobedient and unpredictable, and colors took the brunt of the mistreatment. In the worst cases, everything would look as if it had been through a tumble dryer, its blasé fading an insult to the memory of better times. (In film defender Paul Thomas Anderson's *Boogie Nights* (1997), turning on stock and taking up videotape heralds the beginning of the end for porno's Golden Age on New Year's Eve 1980.) A few brave directors tried their hand at making something of the much-scorned MiniDV aesthetic, films like David Lynch's *Inland Empire* (2006), Spike Lee's *Bamboozled* (2000) and Thomas Vinterberg's *The Celebration* (1998), rappeling into an uncanny valley of not-quite-right color. But armchair enthusiasts simply acclimatized to an inferior standard, helped along by the corresponding blandness of the VHS and Betamax tapes, the earliest media formats offering the mind-boggling capacity to own a movie without a projector.

The upside of a splintering film culture was a big bang for independent cinema, its ideas about color less encumbered by the need for mass appeal enforced by corporate studios. A film like David Fincher's *Seven* (see page 124) had to fight indie distributor New Line Cinema (bought out and shut down by Warner Bros. in 2008) to keep the pitch-black, what's-in-the-box ending, but the broken-glass texture standing in for its vicious pessimism was heartily encouraged. Queer cinema gained traction specifically as a counterpoint to heterosexual squareness, and the unconventional interfacing with color in *Blue* (see page 112) and *But I'm a Cheerleader* (see page 138) followed that punk-ish nonconformist instinct. In need of some buttress to its flagging relevance, Hollywood was sent into an identity crisis. The 1990s began with dressy genuflections to old-school styles—*Dick Tracy* (see page 108) jazzed up pulp and *Schindler's List* (see page 114) channeled the ghost of Michael Curtiz—and ended with leaner updates in chilled colors presaging the digital age to come: 2000 releases *Traffic* (see page 146) and *Gladiator* (Ridley Scott) refreshed the gangster picture and swords-and-sandals epic, respectively.

With the eagle eye of hindsight, we can see how this might be the beginning of the modern cinema business as a constantly shifting hierarchy of power, with upheavals spurred by the technological advances coming with faster and faster frequency. To even the most casual observer, the disparity between the red of 1945 and 1955 is nothing compared with the canyon of difference between the red of 1985 and 1995. At present, the margin of difference is even closer to five years. Soon enough, phases like the videotape era and the boom of diversification it catalysed may collapse altogether. An "of-the-moment" look will last no longer than a moment.

At the risk of posing an obvious question: how do we talk about color? It's hard to quantify "red," for instance, relative to blue, and never mind the difference between scarlet and crimson. The interdisciplinary school of thought known as color theory brings some exactitude to the study of how they're formed, measured, and used in conjunction with one another. Nineteenth-century theorists like Michel Eugène Chevreul and Charles Albert Keeley laid the groundwork by isolating three basic attributes of color: value (which expresses light versus dark), chroma (saturation versus dullness), and hue (the family the color belongs to). Around this time, Keeley made some of the first inroads into avant-garde cinema with his abstract color plates played upon the "magic lantern," the original slide projector. He shied away from narrative in favor of repeating geometrics, wowing incredulous audiences by producing opposite-colored after-images in their eyes once the bulb's light went dark.

All of this is to say that color can provoke an automatic response in the viewer on an involuntary, even biological level, a tenet still widely at play in today's cinema. The very existence of this book is predicated on the idea that filmmakers use color to elicit emotion and signal meaning, but some theory devotees believe that the connection runs deeper and more viscerally than that, going so far as to submit that certain colors can function like a somatic trigger. According to the scientific community, the jury's still out on the legitimacy of "color psychology," with so many personal confounding factors—demographic, upbringing, social environment—making one-to-one connections messy. The blue plate specials in US diners come from the idea that the color blue makes a person hungry, but then so does the ketchup-and-mustard colored branding for burger chains like McDonald's and Wendy's. However unsound, this is a constant in the condensed messaging of marketing; for much of the 2000s, red block letters on a white movie poster denoted a friendly, approachable family comedy in America, while France's equivalent was yellow on blue.

Cinema itself has a sturdier claim to the functioning of color theory in that it generates and operates within its own associations, hardwired into us by a lifetime of media intake. This second-nature encoding predates color coming to cinema in the first place, silent Westerns having ground into viewers that men in white hats are our heroes and men in black hats are bad news indeed. Delineating good and evil wasn't so straightforward after the advent of color, with filmmakers differing on the utility of warm and cool palettes. In *Star Wars*, the light sabers of the peacekeeping Jedi glow blue or green

COLOR
THEORY

The different-colored light sabers in *Star Wars* are used to denote good and evil.

(becalmed inner oneness) while those of the Sith terrorists are red (anger, impulsivity, fire). In millennial successor *Harry Potter*, however, boy wizard Harry's wand emits a red beam of magic (hinting at his lineage of lionhearted nobility) against the dark Lord Voldemort's green (serpentine, posh, poisonous). Drawing sweeping conclusions about colou is a fraught venture if for no other reason than they can mean whatever we want them to.

Lest anyone come away thinking of color theory as hooey, its mapping of the spectrum has more fact-based applications as well. Complements—those colors opposite one another on the Isaac Newton-devised color wheel oriented around the primaries of red, blue, and yellow—contrast with one another to create "color harmony," a satisfying effect that livens up cinematography in

often imperceptible ways. The orange–blue pairing gets the most play—see *Mad Max: Fury Road* (page 188), among countless others—for the inclusion of skin tones within the range of orange and the clean warm/cool polarity between them. That hasn't stopped enterprising filmmakers from dabbling in green–red (as in *God Told Me To*, page 88) and yellow–purple (as in *Black Panther*, page 196). Knowing a color's placement and opposite is the first step to composing a shot's palette, from setting elements in a scene apart from one another to controlling where the audience's eye is drawn. Color theory is just that—theoretical; and in many senses it is unproven, but it is an invaluable intellectual tool. Like everything else at the movies, it's as real as we believe it to be.

ROTTED AMERICANA

BLUE VELVET
DAVID LYNCH
1986

David Lynch traffics in the mixed-up illogic of dreams, under which everything exists in two states at once: the material self, grounded here in the story of a small-town boy stumbling into the seamy underbelly of his sleepy hamlet, and the symbolic self, which appears as the epochal clash between good and evil raging in the film's submerged unconscious. Red-blooded American college student Jeffrey Beaumont finds a severed ear in an overgrown field at one remove from the pristine lawns of Lumberton, and, in search of its owner, he wanders into an off-kilter netherworld of sadomasochism right on top of the one he's always known. As Jeffrey tells Sandy, the girl next door whose wholesome appeal he'll soon outgrow, "I'm seeing something that was always hidden."

With its pliable meanings and free associations, color opens up a trove of possibility for the Lynch's oneiric mode. Red and blue stand in as Manichean opposites splitting the palette into a core duality; their interplay brings the primeval energies warring in the subtext out into Lynch's perversions of film noir and post-war Americana on the exterior. He opens with what may be the definitive picture of prosperity in the U S of A, tilting down from a bluer-than-blue sky to a picket fence as clean and straight and white

as a post-orthodontic smile, with a snatch of pinprick-thorny roses (American Beauties, no less) sprouting in front. The subsequent shots unearth the cannibal insects squirming beneath this well-manicured suburbia, foretelling Jeffrey's descent into the dark, but there's something more sinister than crime festering in Lumberton. What's at stake is humanity itself, Jeffrey's naïveté devoured by swirling malice until he can only cry, "Why is there so much trouble in this world?"

The wayward ear leads Jeffrey to femme fatale Dorothy, who leads him to her psychotic, nitrous-huffing rapist slavemaster Frank Booth. An avatar of pure hatred, he and Jeffrey jockey for the soul of Dorothy, a contest between damnation and salvation that colors her nightclub act. Swathed in blue light against a red curtain, the combo now more sinfully garish than in the opening shot, she's caught in a battle on a cosmic scale. The red curtain reappears in her apartment (and again in Lynch's TV series *Twin Peaks*, which would burrow further into this same thicket of id), where Frank abuses her while Jeffrey watches as a wide-eyed voyeur hiding in the closet. As in a dream, fear can't be fled from, always shapeshifting one step behind our backs.

#445086
R68 G80 B134

#A5CDD9
R165 G205 B207

#9D5468
R157 G84 B104

#281E00
R40 G30 B0

#442D20
R68 G45 B32

#BEA780
R190 G167 B128

#39425F
R57 G66 B95

#BD324C
R189 G50 B76

#CBC5CB
R203 G197 B203

THE TRUE COMIC BOOK MOVIE

DICK TRACY
WARREN BEATTY
1990

Before they were strip-mined for billion-dollar grosses, before they were literature, comic books were thought of as tawdry wastes of time for boys shirking prayer, study, or work. Warren Beatty returned to these halcyon days of funny books with his recklessly over-budget, entirely worth-it adaptation of *Dick Tracy*, the ideal antidote to superhero fatigue. Director and leading man Beatty resolved to stay true to the whiz-bang gestalt of 1930s cartoonist Chester Gould, borne out more in the one-of-a-kind design than in the case that detective extraordinaire Dick is presented with. (The arc daring the serial ladykiller to settle down with a wife and adopted kid was Beatty's self-deprecating send-up of his own serial-monogamist tabloid coverage.)

The character of Dick Tracy was born in a newspaper strip for the *Detroit Mirror*, and soon made his way to books like Dell's *Four Color Comics*, printed using the CMYK method of cyan, magenta, yellow, and the "key" color black created by their overlap. Beatty allowed his production slightly more leeway, assigning the deep-benched creative team seven time-honored colors: red, green, orange, purple, blue, yellow, and pink. Abiding by the parameters of comic printing, these colors were to be unified, with a single agreed-upon shade in costuming and sets from scene to scene. Within those limitations, everyone was encouraged to go wild.

"These are not the kind of colours the audience is used to seeing," remarked cinematographer Vittorio Storaro.

The man who lensed *The Bird with the Crystal Plumage* (1970) for Dario Argento—along with *Apocalypse Now* (1979, Francis Ford Coppola), *The Conformist* (1970, Bernardo Bertolucci), and about a dozen other classics—was at his most liberated under Beatty's advice to do as he will and worry about money later. Storaro tosses off shots his lessers would consider their masterpiece on incidental beats, turning a continuity-maintaining transition of Dick driving away from a crime scene into a phantasmagorical stretch of acidic lime. Richard Sylbert's Oscar-winning set design with decorator Rick Simpson, Milena Canonero's costuming for "Big Boy" Caprice and his grotesque thugs, the fifty-plus matte paintings from visual effects supervisors Michael Lloyd and Harrison Ellenshaw—it is all colored with a joyful sense of abandon, even in a restricted palette. Untethered from anything in the general neighborhood of realism, their style re-establishes that the comic book was meant to be playtime. Beatty and his crack team held themselves to an unbending set of rules, and yet the resultant film makes any gonzo technical wizardry feel possible.

#BE8BB2
R190 G139 B178

#B17F3E
R177 G127 B62

#4965A0
R73 G101 B160

#6A8643
R106 G134 B67

#DF9B92
R223 G155 B146

#3A4164
R58 G65 B100

#82B68D
R130 G182 B141

#7F3D3B
R127 G61 B59

#5D7F59
R93 G127 B89

#49605D
R73 G96 B93

FAMOUS LAST WORDS

BLUE
DEREK JARMAN
1993

In 1974, before London's Tate Gallery was split into the Tate Britain and Modern, the filmmaker Derek Jarman stopped by to see a piece entitled *IKB 79*. The initials stand for International Klein Blue, so named after its creator, French artist Yves Klein, who mixed the color himself and then framed it as a work of art unto itself. It is a blue unlike any other, identifiable by its coordinates of 0-47-167 on the red-green-blue spectrum, and *IKB 79* is one of over two hundred identical paintings by Klein, designed to represent the tone he saw in his mind's eye. He envisioned the lapis lazuli used for the Madonna's robes in medieval paintings, and also ground the pigment aquamarine to stretch for a hue as brilliant as the divine itself. Jarman, likewise moved, would spend the rest of his unduly abbreviated life piecing together how best to bring this transcendent, obliterating blue to the screen.

Over the two decades that followed, he'd fill notebooks with bluisms, sketches, and half-thoughts circling the theme. After Jarman tested positive for HIV in 1986, his sight began degenerating rapidly, and he was stunned to find that everything was fading into the very color that had haunted him all those years. Jolted into action by the finiteness of his remaining time on Earth, he readied his swan song, the seventy-six-minute monologue *Blue*. The film combines a spoken-word piece recited by Jarman and his closest colleagues (including regular muse Tilda Swinton) with an unchanging, unshakable rectangle of IKB from start to finish. The specificity of the color is at odds with its unlimited omnipresence, a blue posited as the all-encompassing essence of everything: death, sex, inspiration, rage, strength, frailty, love.

Jarman's discursive narration holds forth on the indignities of "dying with AIDS" (his preferred phrase, rejecting the upbeat spin of "living with AIDS"), his words now regarded as one of the fundamental first-hand documents of the plague worsened by the UK government's neglect. But it's also his concluding pronouncement as artist, one last offering-up of himself to the gods of color, called out to with the Greek-drama invocation of the opening lines: "O Blue, come forth! O Blue, arise! O Blue, ascend! O Blue, come in!" As everything disintegrated around him, he came to treat good old 0-47-167 as a womb and tomb. When Channel 4 made the momentous choice to run the film free of commercials on television, BBC Radio 3 also simulcast the audio track. Those listeners so compelled could write or call in to the station and request a small lapis-colored card to be held and pondered while listening, a reminder that the visual component isn't just a space-filler. Even when separated, *Blue* and blue were indivisible.

#393C60
R57 G60 B96

HE WHO SAVES ONE LIFE

SCHINDLER'S LIST
STEVEN SPIELBERG 1993

Visualizing the inconceivable horrors of the Holocaust is a high-stakes high-wire act, so much so that a single tracking shot in Gillo Pontecorvo's *Kapò* (1960) earned the director a notorious denunciation in the pages of film journal *Cahiers du Cinéma*. Steven Spielberg was all too aware of what a sensitive assignment *Schindler's List* would be when one of the real-life *Schindlerjuden* approached him in the early 1980s, pitching a biopic of the industrialist responsible for saving a thousand lives under Nazi rule. Having previously made his name excelling in fun for the whole family, Spielberg first offered the script to more mature-minded directors Martin Scorsese, Roman Polanski, and Sydney Pollack, before agreeing to tackle it himself. But once he'd put his mind to it, he vowed to do justice to the largest atrocity faced by the Jewish people since enslavement with a three-plus-hour epic both unsparing and respectful.

This cautious reverence comes through in the cinematography from Janusz Kamiński, his unadorned documentary-style shooting in black and white laying bare the rampant inhumanity of the Third Reich. In contrast to the markedly Old Hollywood chiaroscuro lighting schemes during Oskar Schindler's upper-class hobnobbing, the film refuses to dress up the genocide going on all around

him. With the exception of a prologue and epilogue showing two rites of Judaism—the Sabbath prayer and the laying of rocks on Schindler's actual headstone—Spielberg and Kamiński break with this monochrome scheme on only one occasion. A little girl, portrayed by three-year-old Oliwia Dąbrowska, toddles out of the Kraków Ghetto in a dirtied red coat. It is by this coat that we can identify her again when her body reappears atop a wagonload of corpses exhumed for burning later in the film.

The girl's symbolism can be ascribed easily enough, her cherubic face an emblem of the Jews' annihilated innocence. In Richard Schickel's monograph of Spielberg, however, the filmmaker puts this choice in blunter terms as a comment on America's isolationism in the face of mounting evil: "It was as obvious as a little girl wearing a red coat." In either case, the girl's distinctness is just that—something unique and memorable setting her apart from the gray masses, seen through the eyes of Schindler as he comes to understand the worth of Jewish lives beyond near-free labor. She's a human being, her individuality striking down the wilful vagueness that allows those on the outside to turn a blind eye of ignorance.

 #B95361
R185 G83 B87

 #000000
R0 G0 B0

 #B7B9B4
R183 G185 B180

A TRICOLOR THREEFER

THREE COLORS TRILOGY
KRZYSZTOF KIEŚLOWSKI 1993–1994

One of the most resounding statements on France's national character comes from a Polish-born legend, the reputed pessimist-humanist Krzysztof Kieślowski. His *Three Colors* trilogy organizes itself around the trio of virtues making up the Republic's motto, while making ironic tweaks to the concepts of *liberté*, *egalité*, and *fraternité*. Freedom can be earned only by accepting all that ties us down, equality comes in the form of revenge, and brotherhood flowers in the guarded, somewhat combative bond between a geriatric judge and a comely magazine model. Kieślowski sheds that playful ambiguity in his use of the French flag's striped *tricolore* scheme, which bears significances so profound and glaring as to channel a primal life force.

Starting with their titles, each individual film deploys its given color through avenues either pointed or immersive, but always marked by crucial importance. The first entry, *Blue*, opens with a senseless car crash that leaves Julie (played by Juliette Binoche, pictured) bereft of her husband and son. Although she tries to allay her emotional ruination by cutting herself off from those close to her, the past extends its subtle tendrils back to her in the dashes of sapphire that won't leave her alone. She brings a hanging mobile of blue beads to her new flat as the lone remnant of the one she left behind, and its color leaks into the rest of her life. When most overcome by unspeakable grief, triggered by the music she and her late spouse composed, her vision blues out into a cobalt oblivion.

White finds its defining image in another woman's tender visage—Julie Delpy, resplendent on her wedding day—but tracks the downfall of her soon-to-be-ex-husband, sent by their divorce on a spiral that ends in destitution and desperation. His bleak journey from Paris back to his native Poland moves in shades of off-white matching the dirty snow blanketing his path, a physical layer of depression covering all in sight. His recollection of the wedding day buffs the white to its purest, a snapshot improved through memory, much like the recurring advertisement in *Red* contrasting Irene Jacob's pale complexion against a deep scarlet. She and an older judge strike up a friendship bolstered by their shared yearning for a lasting happiness in their lives, a hard road dotted with noteworthy red props that can tacitly mock or console. In the small universe contained within Kieślowski's France, God works in mysterious ways, but he leaves color-coded hints behind him.

#5496CE
R84 G150 B206

#DAEAED
R218 G234 B237

#3D5794
R61 G87 B148

#DB8AA4
R219 G138 B164

#C94644
R201 G70 B68

#592815
R89 G40 B21

#CCC4BE
R204 G196 B190

#84705C
R132 G112 B92

#90887C
R144 G136 B124

HEARTSICK IN THE CITY

CHUNGKING EXPRESS
WONG KAR-WAI 1994

"All the leaves are brown / and the sky is gray," goes the earworm opener of The Mamas & The Papas' flower-power hit "California Dreamin'." We hear the song over and over in Wong Kar-Wai's romance of missed connections and unrequited crushes, played ad nauseam on a boombox by Faye Wong's pixieish snack stand attendant. Like the song's narrator, she's fleeing her humdrum setting for an idealized getaway flush with color, a trip she first goes on in her mind and then by plane. In the rain-drenched city where Wong sets this downtempo diptych, everyone's looking for a refuge from their longing, each accepting in time that it's not somewhere else, but *someone* else they're really after.

Wong's cinema revolves around relationships too ardent to be put into words; in the heartsick ballad that brought his name to America with help from fan Quentin Tarantino, he dealt with the calibre of unvoiced infatuation in which the sharing of space is all it takes to flood your world with feeling. The industrialized labyrinth of the Lan Kwai Fong neighborhood suffocates with gray, a sea of tin enlivened only by the dim lights of the food kiosks that line its street. When two characters make contact, however, their beat of connection radiates colors Wong

would describe as "sunshiny," "bright," and "lovely." He privileges a cool palette of blues, purples, and toad-hued greens to note the nagging sadness under these encounters—like "California Dreamin'," his sweet song is in a minor key. All the better to play up the moments of unguarded openness, as in the meeting between a jilted cop and a beguiling drug dealer under the orange bulbs of the Bottoms Up Club.

The intimately personal side of color isn't just a key plank in Wong's oeuvre, but in the continuing conversation around it. Between a host of different home-video releases and recutting from distributors for North American markets, his films have more alternate versions than most. For his biggest diehards, the hi-def "World of Wong Kar-Wai" 4K box set from Criterion turned into a sticking point for its reworked look, with contrasts eased up for a more natural finish. The director himself oversaw the adjustments, but a schism still arose between those open to the idea of film as an indefinite, changing entity and those bemoaning the loss of its rough-edged glimmer. Neither *Chungking Express* negates the other, instead leaving us to formulate our own subjective picture of a comforting hideaway no further away than the daydreamed Los Angeles.

 #434970
R67 G73 B112

 #6672A8
R102 G114 B168

 #F3DEA9
R243 G222 B169

#433F2A
R67 G63 B42

#A0793A
R160 G121 B58

#F5E472
R245 G228 B114

#D2704F
R210 G112 B79

#733926
R115 G57 B38

#140000
R20 G0 B0

THE REAL SIN CITY

SEVEN
DAVID FINCHER
1995

There's a thick film of grime, both spiritual and literal, smeared over everything in the anonymous city (in actuality Los Angeles, all identifying marks filed off) stalked by a serial killer in David Fincher's sophomore breakout *Seven*. Filth tones—faecal browns, sooty blacks, vomited greens—have seldom been used to more potent effect than in the fetid crime scenes left behind by the psychopath modeling his gruesome slayings after the seven deadly sins. Most windows have been caked with smudges, painted over, or plastered with newspaper, leaving nude light bulbs or broken wall sconces to cast eerie shadows. Those not blocking out the sun only afford a clearer appraisal of the squalor inside; the long-curdling body of one victim releases a stench so pungent that a canopy of car fresheners can't fully cover it up, the air hanging heavy enough to form a tangible smog a viewer can see in the flashlights' beams.

"Everything is falling apart and nothing is working properly," says production designer Arthur Max, describing the soul-deep disrepair in this dismal any-city. The free-floating malevolence in Darius Khondji's cinematography matches the despair of an outlook founded on near-nihilism, under which the collected cruelties of the human animal put us past the hope of redemption. The mastermind's endgame, more than the racking-up of carcasses, concerns the fallibility of the fresh-faced cop and expectant father played by Brad Pitt; the accumulation of suffering pushes him over the edge and into a decisive act of brutality, leaving him to be swallowed by the degradation he can no longer stave off.

Before forsaking film stock to assert himself as one of the millennium's most tactful digital filmmakers, Fincher capitalized on the reactive properties of his analogue gear. *Seven*'s sandpapery coarseness and high-contrast colors come from a process called bleach bypass, in which the film's silver component is retained during chemical emulsion, essentially generating a black and white image layered over the color exposure. The chilling opening credits sequence, a self-contained companion piece in conception and scoring with the immortally creepy music video for "Closer" by frequent Fincher collaborators Nine Inch Nails, puts this unwell look to expert use on shots of rusted razor blades and needles pulling frayed thread. We see the chapped fingertips of the sadistic John Doe hard at work on his demented projects, perfected by hand—in a twisted way, one dedicated craftsman's nod to another.

#7B9697
R123 G150 B151

#C1C2B3
R193 G194 B179

#42443F
R66 G68 B63

#f6e98b
R246 G233 B139

#858172
R133 G129 B114

#4b3d34
R75 G61 B52

#cdd1ca
R205 G209 B202

#374a58
R55 G74 B88

#171300
R23 G19 B0

BLACKLIGHT POWER MOVEMENT

BELLY
HYPE WILLIAMS
1998

Going by color alone, the most restlessly audacious director in the American cinema has been hiding in plain sight, working in music videos. Hype Williams has racked up hundreds of short-form credits for a murderers' row of rappers, including Tupac Shakur, Missy Elliott, the Wu-Tang Clan—pretty much everyone who's dominated the Top 40 hip-hop charts over the last twenty years. In such recent clips as "Stupid Hoe" for Nicki Minaj or "Marvin & Chardonnay" for Big Sean, Williams lets loose with chroma key lunacy, using green-screen technology to turn the lipstick on Minaj's mouth into an epileptic strobe of neons. The solid-color backgrounds and emphasis on facial close-ups in these late 2010s videos point to an increasing awareness that music videos will be watched on smartphones more often than TVs, but there was a time when his work was permitted to unfurl to its fullest bigness in finer detail.

Permission was in short supply on the set of Williams' first and only narrative feature, however, marred as production was by constant animosity between the director and his producers. Every imaginable calamity conspired to put the shoot behind schedule and over budget, a cast of inexperienced actors prone to showing up late and inebriated not helping matters. Despite an at-times-garbled final product, Williams got away with some flights of stylistic fancy more outré than anything else in cinemas at the time. The film's opening salvos announce its rewriting of the aesthetic rulebook: to the taunting strains of Soul II Soul's "Back to Life," youngblood gangsters Buns and Sin (respectively played by hip-hop prodigies DMX and Nas) stick up a nightclub and seal their fate. As they prowl through the dance floor, ceiling-mounted blacklights make the men look extraterrestrial, their eyeballs glowstick-turquoise against deeper blue skin.

From that point onward, every scene set in a strip establishment would owe a debt to Williams's sui generis hedonism, his impeccable vibe cropping up in unexpected places like Terrence Malick's *Knight of Cups* (2015), Harmony Korine's *Spring Breakers* (2012), or the Safdie brothers' crowd-pleasers *Good Time* (2017) and *Uncut Gems* (2019). Beyond the blacklights, he arranged his frames to highlight one or two dominant colors at a time, an authorial signature carried over from his concept-first approach in music videos. The interdisciplinary mentality he brought to his ill-fated dalliance with moviemaking gave cinema a fresh visual schematic, then got him sent right back to the rap demi-monde, where he was free to promptly resume testing boundaries.

#a5cdd5
R165 G205 B213

#455590
R69 G85 B144

#CDD7EC
R205 G215 B236

#383935
R56 G57 B53

#CD5A57
R205 G90 B87

#492100
R73 G33 B0

FLASH BEFORE YOUR EYES

PEPPERMINT CANDY
LEE CHANG-DONG
1999

In the first of the seven chapters that make up Lee Chang-dong's *Peppermint Candy*, a bedraggled man in a rumpled suit totters over to a picnic by a river. It's his twenty-year class reunion, although everyone's surprised he showed up at all, having been incommunicado since commencement. Visibly distraught, he slurs his way through a couple of minutes of karaoke and then climbs onto some nearby train tracks, screaming "I am going back!" as a locomotive sends him to meet his maker. The other six vignettes give context for this inscrutable tragedy in reverse chronological order, running through the make-or-break points in the life of Yong-ho that tend to favor the "break" side of things. As the narrative structure lifts away his many burdens and self-sabotages one by one, he grows less jaded until we're back at the river's edge twenty years prior, with a laughing Yong-ho oblivious to the hardships he'll soon face.

Made all the more piercing by our painful knowledge of its ending, the film keeps tabs on falls from grace, both Yong-ho's and that of a South Korea plagued by a martial autocracy. While Lee stuck to a naturalistic representation of color that didn't invite as much scrutiny as other aspects of the film, the change from cool to warm tones between the twinned opening and closing scenes summarizes the downward trajectory. The picnic ending in suicide falls on a cloudy day darkening the trees to a deciduous green, whereas the flashback takes place under a sun prettifying the pocket of forest. Yong-ho crawls to his death in a disheveled graphite-gray suit, its formality and flavorlessness a testament to how little their wearer sees life as worth living for. When fresh-faced and well on his way to a degree, Yong-ho wears a brighter blue polo shirt, an accessory to the sadness he releases in a single tear. The blue dress shirt worn under the gray suit intimates that the years have taught him to bury his hurt under a steely outer shell.

His life flowing backward past him, he meanders through broken-down relics of industry dotting Korean towns, mostly in the same decomposing neutral tones seen all over *Red Desert* (see page 58). The amount of time spent among discolored metal stresses the rarity of the woodsy bookends, alive where everything else is dead. Yong-ho returns to the last place he felt something real to end it all, and it's plain to see why he can only be his sincerest self here; after twenty winters, the perennial green always returns, its edges like the walls of a crib he crawls back into.

 #978988
R151 G137 B136

 #D4CEDE
R212 G206 B222

 #8B705E
R139 G112 B94

#425036
R66 G80 B54

TOO COOL FOR SCHOOL

THE VIRGIN SUICIDES
SOFIA COPPOLA
1999

In Sofia Coppola's malaise-terpiece *The Virgin Suicides*, the men raised in a moneyed Michigan suburb relate their boyhood impressions of the five Lisbon sisters, each more ethereal than the last. At one point, they recall obtaining and reading the diary of Cecilia, the first Lisbon girl to take her own life: "We felt the imprisonment of being a girl, the way it made your mind active and dreamy, and how you ended up knowing which colors went together." Style is self for teenagers trying on different identities like clothes in a dressing room, and Coppola's debut feature heeds the importance of surfaces in its meticulously curated aesthetics. In the home of their strict Christian parents, both the color and texture of a saltine cracker, the girls turn their shared bedroom into a bubble of soft lilacs and floral pinks in every shade.

Closed off from the world by their fearful and overprotective parents, the Lisbons collect items that offer a sample of the grown-up femininity that's been locked away from them. Cinematographer Ed Lachman's camera peers at their magpie-like assortment of boutique beauty aids, in colors conjuring an ideal of high-end womanhood out of reach from their gilded cage. But the "oriental" folding fan, the sprays that look like bourbon and white wine, and their screw-on caps have all been washed out to pastels, sapped of their zeal like the downtrodden girls hoarding them. Underlining

the Lisbons' aura of the unknowable by skimping on dialogue, Coppola and Lachman prefer to communicate through full-frame filtering like this. A while after the Lisbons follow through on their suicide pact, a family in the town that has long since moved on from the deaths throws a debutante ball befouled by a smell from a nearby waste spill, and make a laugh of it by choosing a theme for the ball of "asphyxiation"—also the cause of death for middle child Lux. The putrid green gives away the real toxicity, that of the community which choked the life from the girls.

While you'd be hard-pressed to find a single artist more closely identified with Gen X than Sofia Coppola, she also has a legitimate claim to shaping the millennial notion of the "girly." Her read on the meaning of young womanhood as being "all dressed/horned up with nowhere to go" spoke to the incoming generation of internet denizens, who'd remix and revise Coppola's visual autograph online. Amassing pages of jpegs on blogging sites like Tumblr much in the same way the Lisbons stocked their fancy toiletries, users knit the film's faded, powdery colors into their concept of cool. (The shade of salmon termed "millennial pink" oft-seen in advertising and graphic design starts here.) The Lisbon sisters never made it to graduation day, but their sensibility of decoration lives on in any space teenagers are able to make their own.

 #612c29
R97 G44 B41

#7C8BA2
R124 G139 B162

 #364251
R54 G66 B81

 #A38D8F
R163 G141 B143

#6C8354
R108 G131 B84

#333C1A
R51 G60 B26

GIRLS, GIRLS, GIRLS

BUT I'M A CHEERLEADER
JAMIE BABBIT
1999

In Jamie Babbit's queer cult classic set at a conversion therapy camp, the reluctant patients know who they are, their true identities impervious to the compulsory self-denial of "de-gay-ification." Even so, gender and sexuality are articulated through performance—how we dress, the way we stand, our tone of voice—which means that a false persona can be presented just as readily as an honest one. For closeted pom-pom girl Megan, heterosexuality is a disguise she wears until her vegetarianism, Melissa Etheridge CDs and fixation on her teammates' desirous-red miniskirts arouse the suspicions of her conservative parents and boyfriend. They march her off to be brainwashed at True Directions, where the deluded counselors believe that force-feeding her the lies she's been telling herself can eventually make them real.

The staff members (portrayed by Cathy Moriarty and drag icon RuPaul, his casting a dead giveaway to Babbit's campy comedic intentions) assume some formative event turns a child to the path of homosexuality, a psychological misapprehension that also cuts the other way. To steer a youth back toward heteronormativity, they need only reinforce their gender roles by going through the motions. For the ladies, that means vacuuming and other housework, while the fellas butch it up by learning to chop firewood, the gender essentialism driven home by the blue/pink color dichotomy that starts with onesies at birth. Drowning the female attendees in fuchsia Barbie tones is supposed to put them back in touch with their most conventional womanhood; the 1950s kitchenette look harkens back to the all-American nuclear family unit they're being pushed into reproducing.

But the monochromatic interior sets take the pink a step too far into the absurd, and it starts to look more like a parody of itself in line with the satire Babbit has in mind. The irony that gathering hormone-charged teens in closed quarters will only breed more fiery crushes interlocks with a secondary irony: there's something inherently queer about this aggressive playacting of straightness, the paradox on which the Village People's macho-man shtick was built. Staffers like the hunky Rock Brown dress in the obligatory blue tank top to tout their Y chromosomes, but his denim cut-offs and pretty-boy pout make him look like he just stepped out of a gay porno. All the pink meant to blind Megan to herself only brings her confidence in her lesbianism, as she finds love in the feminine crash course counterintuitively trying to stamp it out.

#D37199
R211 G113 B153

#7D7B83
R125 G123 B131

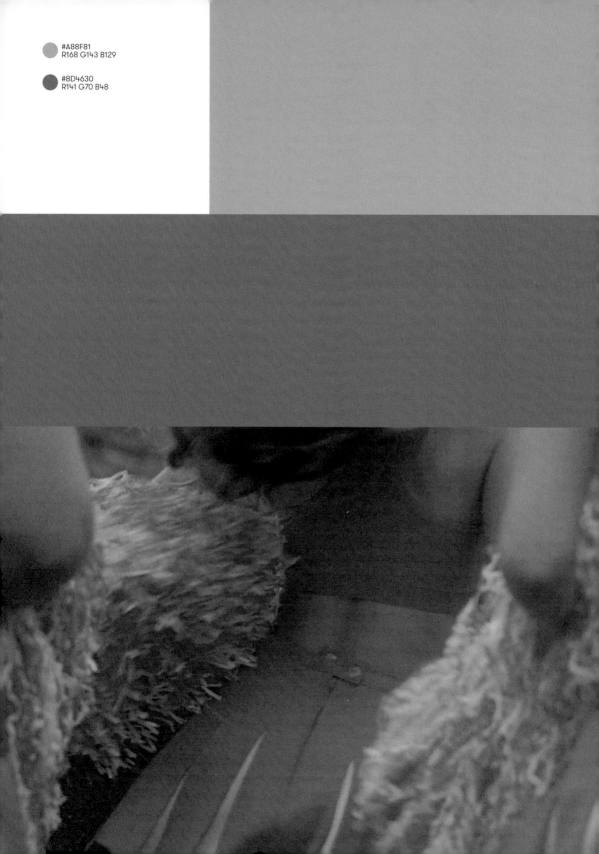

#A88F81
R168 G143 B129

#8D4630
R141 G70 B48

#A98C9F
R169 G140 B159

#986388
R152 G99 B136

GRAY MATTERS

SONGS FROM THE SECOND FLOOR
ROY ANDERSSON
2000

A gray country, Sweden, inside and out. *Songs from the Second Floor*, Roy Andersson's 2000 re-introduction to the arthouse circuit after twenty-five years spent amassing a small fortune from advertising spots and using it to build his own studio in the heart of Stockholm, takes place at the end—of life, of society, of hope. A downtrodden look of defeat has been chiseled into each actor's face, progressively gaunter as they trudge from one miserable humiliation to the next. A crucifix salesman hurls the wares no one's buying into a garbage dump; businesspeople flagellate themselves on the way to the office; passengers lug stacks of baggage to a desolate, beige-lined airport ticketing desk at a slug's pace, spilling golf clubs all over themselves. God has taken leave of these Swedes, who toil in his absence against the uncaring shrug of fate. If not for Andersson's mordant sense of levity, these burnt-out slices of the Sisyphean would be unbearable. But as it is, the slow-moving deadpan plays like a sketch comedy showcase inside an existential black hole.

On his private soundstages, Andersson has the breathing room to do as he pleases, sometimes taking years on end to build his minutely composed shots from the ground up. *Songs from the Second Floor* comprises forty-six such tableaux, all of them static except one, their deep focus so three-dimensional

that "diorama" might be the right word for them. The perfectionist totality with which he designs his moving paintings also covers the color, an all-purpose petrification in the costuming, make-up, and hangar-sized sets. A pervading Scandinavian gray eats away at everything, the characters partially zombified by the pallid foundation pancaked onto their cheeks. The hapless Kalle gets all sooty while rooting around in the charred remains of his furniture store to con an insurance adjuster, the extra shade of dirtiness isolating him from everyone else singing in unison on an overripe-banana-yellow train.

When color does penetrate this force field of desiccated neutral tones, it's still in service of illustrating spiritual malnourishment. The most shocking shot convenes hundreds of onlookers for a solemn ritual in which a young girl is pushed off a cliff to her certain death in a ravine below. The brighter smatters on either side of the frame's sea of dark clothing—the clerics in their baroque robes to the left, and the flag-bearers to the right—jump out, showing how Sweden puts the dignified face of ceremony on the state's reprehensible practices. As glumness oozes from the pores of these sad sacks, they're caught in a drier and more nonchalant variant of the end of days, slowly perishing not in fire and brimstone, but in the dying cinders.

#56595F
R86 G89 B95

#829396
R130 G147 B150

#C2C2C7
R194 G194 B199

#838B93
R131 G139 B147

#6A5147
R106 G81 B71

#3D3F37
R61 G63 B55

#4E5343
R78 G83 B67

#30363B
R48 G54 B59

#8E9EB1
R142 G158 B177

DRUGS, FILTERED

TRAFFIC
STEVEN SODERBERGH
2000

Few directors working in the uppermost tier of Hollywood cultivate such a continuously metamorphosing relationship to the moving image as Steven Soderbergh. A celluloid fetishist who's since embraced lightweight digital shooting, a gearhead at the forefront of feature-length iPhone cinematography, he's exercised this same omnivorous curiosity in his unmistakable color-grading. He's made use of time-saving computer programs during the 2010s to adjust films like *Logan Lucky* or *Magic Mike* to the hue of his liking, but in the crossover smash that earned him the Oscar, he did so using specialized chemical techniques instead of zeroes and ones.

Traffic covers the un-winnable war on drugs from a Dickensian multitude of perspectives, assuming a bird's-eye vantage that includes not just kingpins and police, but also the addicts and politicians subject to the shockwaves of their dirty dealings. Soderbergh keeps his busy plot straight by following *Intolerance*'s example of color-coded organization (see page 18), assigning each piece of the mosaic a discrete visual marker to help audiences along as they sort through a large ensemble. The newly appointed federal drug czar doesn't realize his daughter is freebasing cocaine until she's in the grips of a full-blown sickness, their close-to-home crisis playing out in a cold blue. South of the border in Mexico, the clash between law enforcement and narcos from feuding cartels conveys the relentless rays of the sun with a heatwave of orange. And in southern California, where the wife of a prominent distributor hustles to evade a US Drug Enforcement Administration investigation, the original colors have been intensified rather than redone, reflecting a civilian life turned upside down.

More than just their tint, each narrative strand has a recognizable finish derived from Soderbergh's passion and acumen for film craft, serving as his own cinematographer under his favored pseudonym of Peter Andrews. The specific starkness of the blue comes from tungsten film—meant for indoor photography under tungsten light bulbs, used outdoors in this instance—shot without a filter. A so-called "tobacco filter" produced Mexico's dry amber, with a 45-degree shutter angle exposing each frame to less light for a "strobelike sharp feel." And diffusion filters were the secret ingredient for the SoCal section, overexposing the softened light for what the director calls a "warmer, blossomy feel." He then fed it all through Kodak's Ektachrome film, a higher-speed and simpler-to-process alternative to their famed Kodachrome, for additional contrast upping the appearance of grain. By going the extra mile several times over, Soderbergh set an aesthetic template for criminal grittiness that his many lessers in the genre wouldn't be able to clone.

#CAE1E6
R202 G225 B230

#51726E
R81 G114 B110

#40538F
R64 G83 B143

#616B5F
R97 G107 B95

#F1DFD2
R241 G223 B120

#4B4E57
R75 G78 B87

#90AC8C
R144 G172 B140

#766448
R118 G100 B72

#000000
R0 G0 B0

LA PARISIENNE

AMÉLIE
JEAN-PIERRE JEUNET
2001

On dollars and cents alone, a scant few non-English-language films have achieved the Stateside success of Jean-Pierre Jeunet's sneakily downbeat black comedy. The windfall of profit can be attributed at least in part to the enduring American affinity for Parisian culture, both presented and contradicted through the quirky yet quotidian escapades of one Amélie Poulain, a twenty-something eccentric with a melancholic side to offset her whimsy. Francophiles across the Atlantic fell for what they saw as a picture-perfect rendering of the city, while a faction of critics denounced Jeunet for an overly twee aestheticizing, but they were both slightly off the mark. From the suicide jumper that makes a lifelong impression on a young Amélie by crushing her mother in the opening minutes, Paris is shown to be a more lonely, alienating version of itself than the cute shenanigans involving a garden gnome might suggest.

Jeunet hints at this undercurrent of discontent, the sort of isolation a person only feels when surrounded in a metropolis, with a range of discoloration evoking luscious fruits gone overripe. The dirty textures of his earlier films *Delicatessen* (1991) and *The City of Lost Children* (1995) come creeping back through the vaguely urinary golden filter covering Amélie at the restaurant where she works part time. This yellow establishes itself as the cinematography's neutral tone, tainting what would otherwise be white in outdoor shots, as if the sun's light has curdled. No matter the background color, as in her pomegranate-hued bedroom or against one of the many pea-green walls scattered through the film, the olive-enhanced tone of her skin gives away the persisting presence of that nausea tinge.

Amélie defines herself and the people around her through small pleasures, the all-seeing voiceover blazing through characterization by rattling off a few titbits about a person's favorite smell, preferred TV programmes, or such sensory predilections as fondling dried grains. If this initially seems like an overly precious worldview, the film reveals it to be an expression of Amélie's difficulty connecting to the people around her, who she'd rather engage with via elaborate pranks removing the need for face-to-face contact. Likewise, the Paris she traipses through has a rot underneath its placid surface, beset by attractive colors nonetheless connoting pollution and decay. Jeunet's devious sense of humor, the same that gets a laugh from Amélie's gaslighting torment of one man to the brink of sanity, turns its visual representation into a bait-and-switch at the expense of the cinema-going tourist's imagined France.

 #753930
R117 G57 B48

#6C733B
R108 G115 B59

 #DFC85F
R223 G200 B95

#596443
R89 G100 B67

#363309
R54 G51 B9

#923F38
R146 G63 B56

#593C1F
R89 G60 B31

#EDD75D
R237 G215 B93

#923F38
R146 G63 B56

INTO THE GHIBLIVERSE

SPIRITED AWAY
HAYAO MIYAZAKI
2001

Hayao Miyazaki has secured his place on anime's Mount Rushmore, the uniformly superb productions from his Studio Ghibli having a major hand in adding Asian animation to the American moviegoing palate. The ones he directed, most hallowed among them *Spirited Away* (then the highest-grossing Japanese movie ever), lead us into a Ghibliverse gentler and kinder than our own. Food looks tastier, water looks fresher, and —although fear can encroach on the sense of childlike wonder the camera shares with plucky Chihiro—the forests and grasslands she passes through look prettier. On the drive to their new home, she and her parents stop by a shrine long since reclaimed by vines. Their car, a gray hunk of machinery outlined in black, stands out against the unlined trees and bushes painted in sun-dappled greens.

A long-time environmentalist, Miyazaki positioned his Academy Award-winning fairytale as a defense of the planet we've been taking for granted when not outright abusing. Chihiro's parents turn into screeching pigs as a warning against consumerist gluttony; a glop-monster is actually a river spirit contaminated by pollution; another personified river develops amnesia after apartment developments are built over his banks. The director's cosy sensibility of color gets across his love of Mother Earth by basking in the hushed tranquillity of rural

Japan, and its meadows still unsullied by human meddling. While Chihiro formulates a plan to save her mum and dad, she finagles some short-term employment at a spirit-world spa accessible by a train with tracks running over a riverbed that floods daily. On what looks like the most clement afternoon of the year, its clouds shifting to the purple-orange that foreshadows a great sunset, a wide shot of the train gliding over the water shows humanity and nature in peaceful harmony.

In Japanese culture, clouds are symbolically linked with the blooming of *sakura* (known also as cherry blossom), the fleeting prime of which also represents the impermanence of all earthly things. This concept is summed up in the untranslatable phrase *mono no aware*, the closest thing to a moral that Chihiro takes away from the bedtime story she's living out. While cavorting about with her enigmatic friend Haku, she's wreathed in an arresting shot by a bushel of cherry blossoms in a blush of pink, their soothing petals a sign that she's turning over a new leaf of her own. She's loath to relocate to an unfamiliar town in the opening scenes, and by the final shots, she's acquiesced to life's constant moving on. Nothing lasts forever, although Miyazaki still takes a small comfort in the assurance that his lovingly illustrated rocks and streams will be here long after we're gone.

#DCAAA8
R220 G170 B168

#D57B65
R213 G123 B101

#68723C
R104 G114 B60

#6072A8
R96 G141 B168

#E4AB93
R228 G171 B147

#CBA959
R203 G169 B89

4

DIGITAL
WONDERLANDS

Ang Lee's *Life of Pi* shows what digital cinema can accomplish, for example this CGI sunset.

The computer has done more than any single invention—and that includes the camera—to shape the modern film industry, completely overhauling how movies are shot, edited, sold, promoted, and watched. With the benefit of an ever-growing hindsight, it's becoming clear that the history of the moving picture will be cleaved in half, not by the addition of sound or color but by digitization, which radically altered both. Affordable consumer-grade DSLR cameras, as well as software like Final Cut and Premiere, allow hobbyists to produce independent work that more closely resembles professional filmmaking than a home movie; but some intangibles have been lost along the way. The texture of a digital film—itself an oxymoronic phrase nonetheless accepted into the common lexicon—just isn't the same as its analogue forebear's, and nowhere is that difference more pronounced than in their respective expressions of color.

Instead of exposing the light taken in through the lens directly onto a filmstrip, the latest digital cameras use a sensor chip to translate that light into millions of pixels then preserved on a hard drive's data bank. The driving concept behind the technology is the pursuit of uniformity and consistency, divorced from the fragile variance of the exposure process and the wear and tear of projection. While digital footage could be stored and electronically transported without crackles, pops, scratches, or other distortions, those imperfections bore a worn-in charm lost in the sterile, razor-sharp aesthetic of computerized cinema. Too many of the big-budget releases in today's cineplexes settle for an unsightly washed-out palette or an artificially sweetened one, a Hobson's choice between moldering grayish-blues and a screensaver sheen in which the only thing really being offered is falsity.

Although Instagram filters and the like attempt in vain to mimic the organic cosiness of celluloid, the most innovative works of this era come from artists and technicians figuring out how to make that synthetic quality work for them. In some cases, as in the polarizing post-millennium output of Michael Mann, this means fully embracing the smeary motion and shallow blacks endemic to the video equipment in use and then challenging the public to adapt. Ang Lee has spent his last few features charting the limits of what digital cinema can accomplish, from the auto-tuned oranges in the CGI sunsets of *Life of Pi* (2012) to test trials with muddy, high-framerate photography in *Billy Lynn's Long Halftime Walk* (2016) and *Gemini Man* (2019). Whether these experiments have been successful is another matter entirely, but all the same, they represent an earnest endeavor to conceive of what cinema's next evolutionary phase might look like.

Other specimens have occupied this virtual mode from a stance of ironic or at least knowing remove, commenting on the brave new world they have no choice but to inhabit. An increasing number of blockbusters go to great pains to obscure their nonreal environs, cloaking the green screens and motion capture with a click here and there. The best among them turn this phenomenon in on itself, poking fun at or reveling in the thin façade covering the foundation of ones and zeroes. While some celluloid loyalists continue to hold fast to the traditions of old, more intrepid forward thinkers have devised ways of replicating other mediums, such as comic books or video games, while conceding the dissimilarity between digital and analogue forms. The computer's rise to dominance now amounts to a tricky, almost untrustworthy cinema, in which the colors presented to us shine brighter than ever, albeit with their origins hidden. The crimsons and chartreuses could either be an incredible find by the location scout or retouching from the editor—or a mirage conjured from scratch.

In the first week of November 1953, the Radio Corporation of America (RCA) gathered producers from Hollywood's top studios at the National Broadcasting Company's (NBC) lot in Burbank, California to behold the vision of their demise. Everyone sat for a half-hour programme, part pre-recorded and part live, and made history along the way by watching the first coast-to-coast broadcast of color television. David Sarnoff, Chairman of the Board at both RCA and NBC, proudly informed his competition that consumer-friendly color TV sets were on track to be rolled out within the next two or three years. The unspoken message of his dog and pony show was hard to miss: small screens were catching up to the large. If he had his way, the days of the movies would be numbered.

"The cold fact is that color television, even in its present experimental stage, is the equal, when seen under ideal circumstances, of the best quality color movies to be seen in theaters," wrote *The New York Times*'s Thomas M. Pryor in a report from the scene of Sarnoff's show-off. He made this declaration with a strange air of finality, proven misplaced by the following seventy years of hot-blooded debate over the merits and detriments of public versus home viewing. Every other month, social media lights up with volleys from extremists on either side of the aisle, insisting on the sanctity of the auditorium's temple or the superiority of the living room entertainment center. The correct take lies somewhere in the middle, near the compromise that each has its place. The silence, darkness, and size of the movie theater remains the only way to feel the full impact of a film, while televisions have the advantage of convenience on nights when we don't feel like shelling out for tickets.

But the color TV has stayed hot on the trail of the perfection Pryor saw in a device that would be considered hilariously obsolete by today's standards. In the 1950s, the ability to transmit three monochrome images in red, blue, and green layered over each other by a cathode ray tube—the "dot-sequential" system developed by the RCA-owned NBC and the National Television System Committee formed for the purpose—was a mind-blowing marvel. Once RCA's per-unit manufacturing costs sank and in-color programming proliferated in the early 1960s, NBC hurried to cater to the influx of buyers with income to afford the top of the line. Disney renamed

THE COLOR TV

The colorful uniforms of *Star Trek's Enterprise* crew, designed to show off color TV's abilities.

its long-running anthology series *Walt Disney's Wonderful World of Color* and left ABC; the first episode of its NBC run featured Donald Duck's haughty German uncle Ludwig von Drake giving a lecture in song on the bullet points of color theory. Network notes on the pilot of *Star Trek* called for more color to move RCA's products, hence the red, yellow, and blue uniforms on the starship *Enterprise's* crew, and the redesign of the space-age-gray bridge set with livelier railings, panels, and warning lights.

TV's chase for the standard of brilliance set by the cinema went on and on, the transition to digital broadcasting accelerating the arms race. Each successive model claimed

to be the killer tech that would finally render moviegoing a thing of the past with its crystal clarity, from the short-lived plasma screen to the liquid-crystal display to the organic light-emitting diode in common use today. HD, 4K—we constantly invent new language to measure the sharpness and the depth of color attainable within the home, keeping pace with cinematic advancements like IMAX or American bricks-and-mortar chain Regal's in-house branded version RPX. Try as it may to extinguish its silver-screened nemesis, the color TV still can't supersede the genuine article of cinema, even as it's taken over the world.

MAKING 'EM LIKE THEY USED TO

THE AVIATOR
MARTIN
SCORSESE
2004

In America or elsewhere, living or dead, there's no filmmaker with deeper cinephile bona fides than Martin Scorsese. The history of the medium courses through his work, not just in the homages to his eclectic range of favorites—Powell and Pressburger, Kurosawa, Méliès, and many others dissected in this book—but in his undying fascination with the malleability of the filmed image. In this period epic tracking the most eventful years of obsessive-compulsive tycoon Howard Hughes, Scorsese shot on film and played with digital post-production programs to revive long out-of-date color formats. As the "boy genius" ploughs through the early decades of Hollywood and elbows his way to the front of the business, the means by which he's depicted also progress in tandem with the times.

Hughes threw a chunk of his considerable fortune behind a couple of small-time directors named Rowland V. Lee and William Worthington, the originators of Multicolor, one of the bipack "two-strip" colorizing processes at the cutting edge of the early 1930s. A pair of filmstrips would run superimposed over each other, one capturing red dye and the other cyan, the rudimentary two-color display still a high-tech step up from

black and white for the amazed audiences. In the first fifty-two minutes of his film, Scorsese apes this archaic method with the help of a 3D lookup table, a computer graphics processor converting the "color space" of a frame into a spreadsheet of numerical values allowing for pinpoint analysis and alteration. When Hughes crash-lands his aeronautical pride and joy, the H-1, in a beet field following a test flight, the vegetables have that burnished red against the leaves' counterbalanced cyan, the same hue as the off-color peas he's served at a dinner a few scenes later.

Once the timeline hits 1935, Scorsese shifts gears into three-strip Technicolor befitting the setting, an explosion of saturation all the more noticeable for its previous absence. We can share in the revelatory awe moviegoers of the day would've experienced, witnessing the birth of full color in the idyllic green of the Hepburn family compound or the bathroom Hughes's germophobia won't let him exit. Unafraid of the future while reverent of the past, Scorsese directs the tools of modernity to the cause of classicism, upholding the rarefied grace of old-fashioned film aesthetics without actually doing it the old-fashioned way.

 #2D3715
R45 G55 B21

 #4B4033
R75 G64 B51

 #6A9D69
R106 G157 B105

#C6C8DB
R198 G200 B219

#A73D38
R167 G61 B56

#75B3C4
R117 G179 B196

#393B2F
R57 G59 B47

#AFC85D
R175 G200 B93

#45472F
R69 G71 B47

#6D6D72
R109 G109 B114

DIRTY GAMES

SAW II
DARREN LYNN
BOUSMAN
2005

4 Digital Wonderlands

Jean-Luc Godard famously mused that all you need to make a movie is a girl and a gun; the *Saw* films countered with two guys and a bone saw. The first in the long-running mutilation-palooza did a lot with a little, chaining a pair of unfortunates in a locked room and gauging how much pain they'd be willing to take if it meant walking away with their lives. But the series really came into its own with the superlative second instalment, which cracked the formula that would see deranged puppet-master Jigsaw through: you need a whole group of people, in a setting large and varied enough to contain a full smorgasbord of torture devices. Moreover, director Darren Lynn Bousman found a look that wouldn't just set the course for the rest of the *Saw* outings, but for a generation of bloodthirsty horror films jacking their swagger.

The new face of excruciation would be green, as if liable to retch at any moment. Bousman and cinematographer David A. Armstrong doubled up by color-grading on top of the painted walls of Jigsaw's skin-flensing playhouse, both in a wormed-over hunter's green calling to mind all manner of unsavory things—spoiled food, diseased phlegm, the stuff that might build up around an infected papercut. As a diss from opponents and praise from the faithful, the *Saw* films have been called a wallow in

gratuitous depravity, and its end goal of immiseration dictated the queasy putrescence of its colors. More than scary, the set pieces involving wrist-shredding razor blades or a pit of hypodermic needles are just hard to watch. The most unappealing public-toilet green available was only apropos.

The year 2005 saw the release of both *Saw II* and Eli Roth's *Hostel*, two nasty pieces of work which jointly formed the vanguard of the horror subset "torture porn," collecting the films that lavished grueling punishments upon murder-fodder for our sick amusement. Through the 1980s and 1990s, slasher stars like Jason Voorhees and Freddy Krueger took the precedent of Herschell Gordon Lewis's splatter cinema in a poppier direction, melding the strawberry tones of its blood with a studio-subsidized polish. On the other amputated hand, the jets of rotten maroon spurting out of Jigsaw's prey barely look like they've come from a human body. *Seven* (see page 124) was the disrupting factor in the progression of horror, its disgusting atmosphere driven even deeper into obscenity. The bleach bypass that David Fincher drove himself up a wall to get just right had been replaced by a quicker, cheaper, and meaner form of filth. The genre was subsumed by this unholy green, like it was sinking into a poisonous swamp.

#3F4621
R63 G70 B33

#B5BA65
R181 G186 B101

FASTER THAN REALITY

SPEED RACER
LANA & LILLY WACHOWSKI
2008

An audiovisual overload designed to singe your eyeballs to a crisp, a dynamo of limitless propulsive energy, the possible final form of the cinematic medium or perhaps its death knell—it's difficult not to talk about the Wachowski sisters' take on this Japanese pop-culture sensation in hyperbolic terms, if only because it's a hyperbolic movie by nature. The rambunctious youngster named Speed Racer will settle for nothing less than being the greatest automobile driver who ever lived, which means going faster than anyone has gone before on courses that leave the laws of physics in the dust. And the scenes in between the high-octane set pieces don't let up on the throttle, every exchange of dialogue or solitary pensive pause cranked into the red with an array of CGI amazements.

Lana Wachowski has named James Joyce's stream-of-consciousness prose and the irreverent reconfigurations of the Cubists as influences on this anything-goes aesthetic mêlée, in which the styles of the source anime and manga collide with children's doodles, kung fu B-movies and a computerized hyperrealism. The deliberateness behind the artificiality (which turned off critics and viewers in 2008, unprepared for its candy-fuelled assault on the senses) is most evident in the over-the-top color palette, its saturation levels as high as the post-production team could take them. When Speed bursts out of a day at school to meet big brother Rex in a flashback, the pure green-screen environment presents a heightened outdoors in which the sky is too blue and the trees are too green. The Wachowskis broke barriers by leaning into the uncanniness, polishing their imagery to a plastic shine that makes everything resemble a toy-version of itself.

The directors get their biggest kicks through the kaleidoscopic maximalism of the racing scenes, in which the whiplash-inducing velocity leaves light and color rushing to keep up. As Speed diagonally drifts across a strip of raceway, the pattern on the road is blown away behind him like a sand mandala; in the orgasmic finale of the all-the-marbles Grand Prix, Speed's 360-degree spin across the finish line briefly sucks him into a spiral of red chequers. (This, after busting through a multicolor, multi-car explosion plucked right from *2001: A Space Odyssey*—see page 66.) Rather than providing a shortcut, the up-to-the-second CGI technology allowed for more complicated, intricate, and altogether more laborious production design. Like the tricked-out hot rod piloted by Speed, the camera can seemingly be made to pull off any stunt.

 #4A4A24
R74 G74 B36

 #2D1300
R45 G19 B0

 #CB4F4D
R203 G79 B77

#ACA9CD
R172 G169 B205

#C63D3A
R198 G61 B58

#465692
R70 G86 B146

#698442
R105 G132 B66

THE NEXT LIFE

ENTER THE VOID
GASPAR NOÉ
2009

Never one for subtlety, French enfant terrible Gaspar Noé lays out the basis for the scandalizing work of surrealism he has in store with the singular *Enter the Void* through a characteristically heavy-handed exchange of dialogue near the top. A burnout explains to his pill-pushing acquaintance Oscar that as the body readies for death, the brain releases the same neurochemical activated by the acid-on-acid hallucinogen known as DMT. "It's a little like dying would be the ultimate trip," he says, as close to a mission statement as Noé could get. Oscar will soon be sent to a premature grave by a policeman's bullet. Once he does, we'll inhabit his displaced soul's perspective as it floats around Tokyo to check in on his loved ones, dipping in and out of the afterlife's murky psychoactive soup as he goes.

He does so with the bleary-eyed philosophizing of a first-semester undergrad, but Noé took it upon himself to answer the intimidating question of what death looks like, an inquest leading him along some fantastical, colorful tangents. Prior to shuffling off this mortal coil, Oscar already leads a life lending itself to an overdrive of stimuli not far removed from the posthumous bath of sensation awaiting him. His squalid, economical Japanese apartment faces a dive

bar's sign, which fills his balcony and living room with a rotation of grubby, casino-ish color. The oscillations make for good zone-out ambience while getting high, as when he smokes a hit of DMT and falls into the abstract maw that materializes on his ceiling. Having been around the recreational narcotic block a few times in his day, Noé drew on his own tripping (as well as the nineteenth-century biologist-artist Ernst Haeckel's illustrations of wriggling amoebas in *Art Forms of Nature*) for the designs of the CGI fractals that shift between fleshy shades of red at the same slow pace as the sign outside.

These overtures prepare us for the provocations to come once Oscar goes to the other side. Sometimes, the screen blinks stroboscopic between red and white, as if glitching out in an effort to be both colors at once. In the looping crane shots over Tokyo's love hotels and strip clubs, Oscar sees through an opened third eye, the genitals of couples locked in coitus pulsating with a visible charge. In death, he gravitates toward clusters of blacklight, stopping to visit the memory of a friend's model of Tokyo doused in phosphorescent purple. On this vicarious voyage through the great beyond, we're free to drink in the neon-laced purgatory overlaid on our reality.

#5F74AB
R95 G116 B171

#C5383C
R197 G56 B60

#CC4384
R204 G67 B132

#63A051
R99 G160 B81

#9A3B31
R154 G59 B49

#391800
R57 G24 B0

#A4B7A3
R164 G183 B163

#864060
R134 G64 B96

TERROR IN R/G/B

AMER
HÉLÈNE CATTET &
BRUNO FORZANI
2009

All of creation lies somewhere between red, green, and blue. The commonly used additive model of color combines these three foundational bases in varying intensities to create every speck of the rainbow, white being the point of equilibrium between them. (The trusty three-strip Technicolor process made use of the inverse "subtractive" CMYK model also used in printing.) Up to the late twentieth century, cameras would use prisms to separate incoming light into individual tubes holding the red, green, and blue (R/G/B) components. Press your face up against an older television set or computer monitor, and you'll see that each pixel is made up of three minuscule lights in that same inescapable grouping. This goes all the way back to the cones of the human retina; we were the first prototype for this technology.

Amer, the first feature from Belgian husband-and-wife formalists Hélène Cattet and Bruno Forzani, pushes the leering lechery of Dario Argento and his slasher pictures classified as thrillers or *giallo* (yellow) even further out there. The tripartite coming of age for French Riviera girl Ana, from child to teen to woman with three different actors, barely has any dialogue and only the faintest wisp of a plot. All insert shots and disembodied close-ups, its violence comes from everywhere and nowhere, like knockout gas. Cinema itself becomes an expansive arsenal of weaponry, rapid-fire cuts slashing through supple flesh and leaving gashes deeper than a knife's. In their most jarring attack, Cattet and Forzani break down a series of shots into their R/G/B elements and play them sequentially, ripping the body apart with a vivisection on the subatomic level.

The deconstructed colors hit as the youngest Ana peeps in on her parents *in flagrante delicto*, the trauma all children must confront sooner or later in what Freud called "the primal scene." As she comes to grips with the erotic neuroses switched on from within the horror and confusion, the lurid reds, greens, and blues follow her with the same menace as the veiled specter that roves through her home. Complemented by a hot pink signifying the instability she's added to the rancid psychological stew inside her, the three elemental colors terrorize her right up to the precipice of death. Forzani and Cattet would reprise their R/G/B experimentation a few years later with their short film *O Is for Orgasm*, a contribution to the omnibus horror collection *The ABCs of Death* (2012). Like Ana, maybe they're also cursed to see that ever-present building-block color scheme in everything and everywhere.

● #2A273C
R42 G39 B60

● #4A5D98
R74 G93 B152

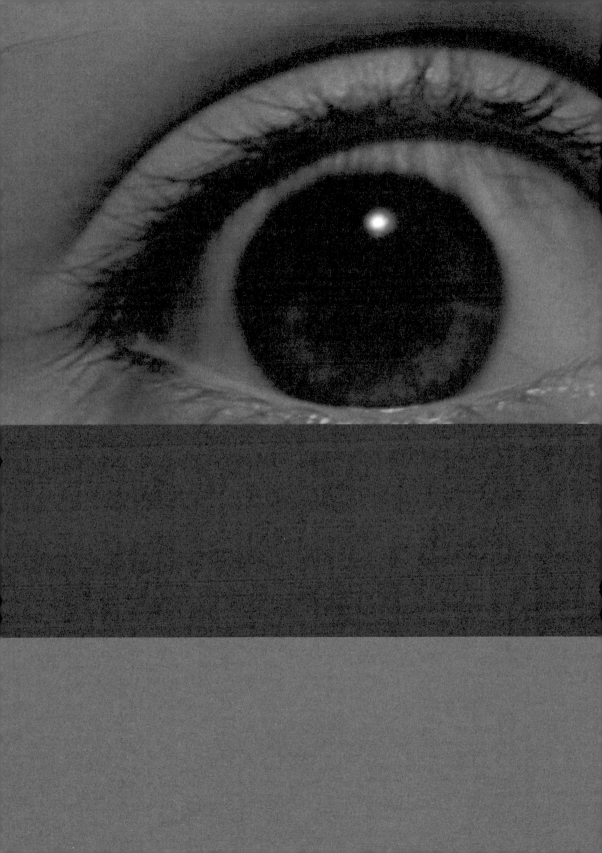

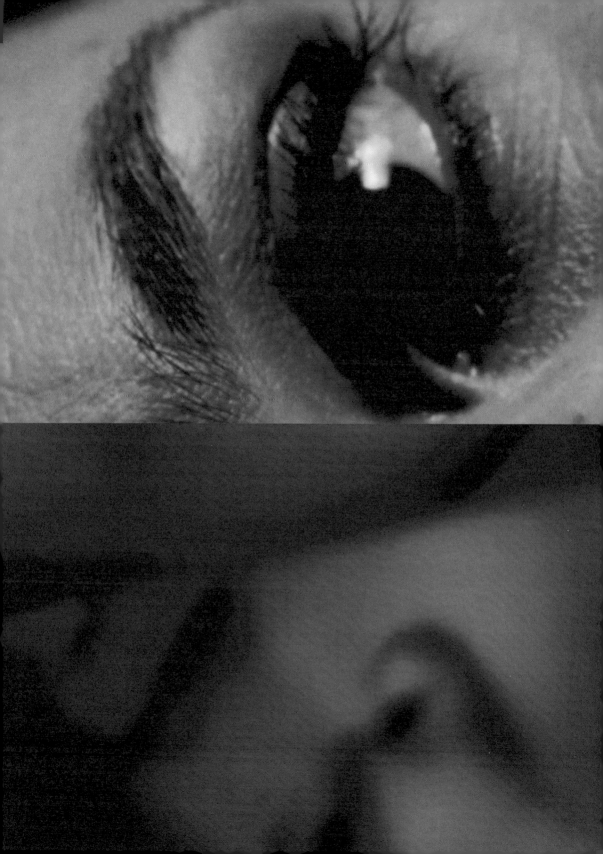

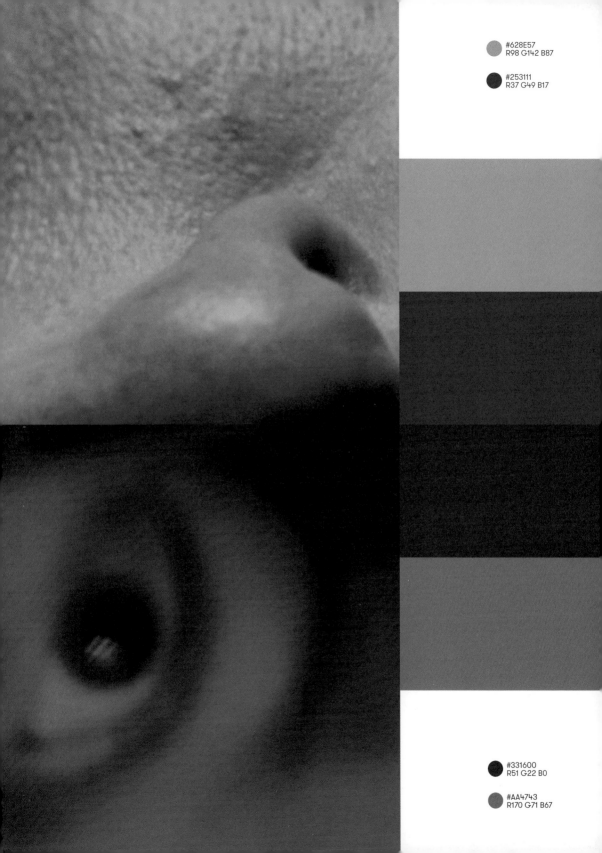

#628E57
R98 G142 B87

#253111
R37 G49 B17

#331600
R51 G22 B0

#AA4743
R170 G71 B67

COMPUTERIZED NIGHT

TRON: LEGACY
JOSEPH KOSINSKI
2010

When Disney approached special effects guru Joseph Kosinski with an offer to get into feature directing—whip up a sequel to the 1980s kitsch object *Tron*, updated for a post-*Matrix* industry paradigm—he said he'd do it, but only if he could do it his way. The teeming cyberspace of the Wachowski sisters' sci-fi dystopia (see page 168) didn't interest Kosinski, nor did the internet itself; instead, he took cues from automotive design and his own academic background in architecture for a virtual universe forgotten by time. The film sends hero Sam Flynn into the video game mainframe designed by his father in the original film, a negative zone known as The Grid that's now been sequestered offline for thirty years and "evolved on its own" like a "virtual Galapagos," as the first *Tron*'s director Steven Lisberger (a producer on the sequel) explained. "It doesn't have that Pong Land vibe to it anymore."

While maintaining the clean, straight lines and streakless surfaces of its context in video gaming, the franchise leapt forward in overall sophistication, its soundstage sets of concrete, glass, and steel augmented by pixel-storm backgrounds. Kosinski's chief stroke of inspiration was to take up black as his neutral base tone, submerging his chilly datascapes in a void flatter and sleeker than mere darkness. With no sun or moon to speak of, the only light comes from what

the objects in a scene can emit, such as the skintight super-suits outfitted with flexible polymer lamps colored in an otherworldly orange or blue by a homemade vinyl finish. Lit from below with glowing floors often kept out of the frame, all characters have a phantom gauntness about their faces, a nocturnal pulchritude unseen in any studio production since.

Upon its theatrical run in 2010, Kosinski's mad vision of a tucked-away arcade universe was met with mixed reviews for the—fairly noted—bloat in its script. The speechifying about Christ complexes and creation myths may very well be a bunch of "bio-digital jazz," to borrow a phrase from Jeff Bridges, reprising his role from the first film as programmer Kevin Flynn, now deified as the lord of this realm. But this dissonance between superior technical might and substandard storytelling marks this film as typical of its epoch in Hollywood, when event releases such as this often serve as scaffolding on which to hang some CGI. But there's a daring design to Kosinski's auspicious debut absent from comparable shock-and-awe bonanzas like *Avatar* (James Cameron, 2009). Beneath the theological hot air, beneath all the money, there's a fastidious stylist and his drive to create something novel from an assignment of leftover intellectual property.

#DC925A
R220 G146 B90

#A1CBD2
R161 G203 B210

#2C3536
R44 G53 B54

#2C3635
R44 G54 B53

#CE664A
R206 G102 B74

#F3D46D
R243 G212 B109

#272F31
R39 G47 B49

#E0EEF6
R224 G238 B246

#77A4B7
R119 G164 B183

THE AESTHETE'S SWEET

THE GRAND BUDAPEST HOTEL
WES ANDERSON
2014

His detractors like to believe Wes Anderson is all surface and no depth, an aesthete obsessed with style at the cost of the soul that should be animating it. But his films have always attended to some deeper emotional wound, forever mourning the broken relationships between parents or siblings or children or lovers. His latest phase has expanded this intimate vulnerability to national proportions, charting the spread of authoritarianism through postcard caricatures of countries in Asia—as in *Isle of Dogs* (2018)—and Europe—as in *The French Dispatch* (2021) and *The Grand Budapest Hotel*, the most ambitious of this globetrotting period. Through decades-spanning frame stories within frame stories, we learn of the once-august haven for travelers in the fictitious Alpine nation Zubrowka, an invention inspired by the works of Austrian novelist Stefan Zweig. By the 1980s, the outermost timeframe of the film's nested structure, the now much less-frequented stopover has been redesigned as a gray, borderline-brutalist shell of its former glory. The main narrative picks up in 1932 and returns the bustling edifice to its prime, when it popped out as a splash of bubblegum-pink against the majesty of the purple mountains surrounding it.

An oasis of amenities, the hotel comes to embody civility, pleasure, and all the other precious things that would be lost in the barbarism of the impending world war. Anderson uses color to signify this type of human currency, outfitting head of staff M. Gustave and lobby boy Zero in grape-tone uniforms that mesh harmoniously with the red of the elevator, the orange of the lobby, and the blue of the spa. (Real-life photos of the latter location reveal that Anderson tinkered with the footage's color-grading to give the space a warmer energy the approximate shade of melted sorbet.) The hotel's pink also matches that of the *courtesan au chocolat*, a pastry delicacy whipped up by Zero's baker girlfriend Agatha.

Beauty and taste connect people through a shared dignity; M. Gustave is part of a clandestine society of hotel operators that look out for and defend one another, each member attired in a snappy monochromatic ensemble. When the forces of fascism rear their ugly heads, they bring brusqueness and greed and violence, but the surest sign of their evil is the black clothing that ink-stains Anderson's world. For all the dead bodies the jackbooted "ZZ" soldiers leave in their wake, their true offence is drabness.

 #E3A9BA R227 G169 B186

 #8B7074 R139 G112 B116

 #D8826B R216 G130 B107

 #526284 R82 G98 B132

#D38468
R211 G132 B104

#C29287
R194 G146 B135

#59484D
R89 G72 B77

PEDAL TO THE METAL

MAD MAX: FURY ROAD
GEORGE MILLER
2015

Sometimes, seizing inspiration is a matter of recognizing the presiding zig of the pop-cultural moment and zagging as hard as humanly possible in the opposite direction. George Miller's series of unleaded motor operas roared back onto the scene after a three-decade hiatus to find post-apocalyptica overrun by *The Hunger Games* and its innumerable bastard offspring scurrying underfoot. Surveying the genre and seeing nothing but corpse tones, he issued a simple directive to Eric Whipp, the senior colorist, which he recalls as "it should be saturated and graphic, and the night scenes should be blue." During his time spent on the job, Whipp gave himself the secondary guideline to "make it look like a graphic novel," a succinct summary of the white-knuckle kineticism crackling in every frame.

The coupling of orange and teal had ossified into cliché through scores of one-sheet posters and action tentpoles, but Miller and Whipp brought the scheme back to life with a stylistic electro-shock. The film's threadbare plot, which comprises little more than a single day's drive across a stretch of desert and back, is divided into three movements. The first depicts the full force of the heatwave that's sent the Earth into an eternal drought, everybody's agonizing thirst translated into a sunburned sand so atomic-tangerine that it seems to tint the sky above it. The conditions are unforgiving—"out here, everything hurts," growls the hardened Furiosa—but it's still a lovely day for the end of the world. The digitally sharpened orange/teal contrast between the sparsely populated ground and lip-chapping air, often perfectly bisecting a frame, proves that lifelessness needn't equate to listlessness.

The second movement takes place that night, shot during a cloudy Namibian day with shadows re-inserted after the fact, exposing details hidden by the dark yet vibrant blue that Miller had specified. (The near-monochrome coloration of this segment calls into question the necessity of the grayscaled Black and Chrome cut released on video for mega-fans, a winnowing-down of something already honed to its core.) The final third starts after dawn on a morning made overcast during post-production, with the characters still lit by full daylight to pop them out against the ominous background. Across all three, the brash color-grading and quieter CGI modulations work toward the overarching goal of replenishing the barren hellscapes of a depleted genre. The film ends with Furiosa opening the floodgates to release life-giving water, an image not so far from Miller's benevolent restoring of color to our on-screen Armageddons.

 #795229
R121 G82 B41

#DD9256
R221 G146 B86

 #587A8E
R88 G122 B142

#C6CEE6
R198 G206 B230

#5478AF
R84 G120 B175

#2F3749
R47 G55 B73

#3F3A29
R63 G58 B41

#3E5652
R62 G86 B82

#DA8736
R218 G135 B54

ONCE MORE, WITH FEELING

LA LA LAND
DAMIEN CHAZELLE
2016

Damien Chazelle worships music as a real thing and idea, both the pleasing noise of it and everything else it entails: its theory and mechanics, the dingy clubs it gets jumping and—more than anything—the frustrated strivers playing its notes. The indie stalwart's first shot at an all-the-trimmings studio picture wasn't just an original musical— among the last of a dying breed—but a meditation on the genre, a valentine to it, and a eulogy for it. Art's not in great shape around Chazelle's Los Angeles, where talentless phonies score fat contracts while artists starve in obscurity. Pasadena's Rialto movie palace hosts an early date between jazz-fiend pianist Seb and out-of-work actress Mia, its later closure (the site is now a non-denominational church) a metaphor for their crumbling relationship and the state of showbiz that atrophies along with it.

Even if Chazelle didn't tuck a French *parapluie* shopfront into a scene set on the Warner Bros. lot (or name the main characters of his first film Guy and Geneviève), the influence of *The Umbrellas of Cherbourg* (see page 54) on him would be undeniable. He and Jacques Demy are kindreds in their hopeless-romantic belief that life is full of marvellous things too good to last, and they manifest it through the same spritzes of friendly primary color. In the

gauntlet-throwing opening number, Angelenos emerge from a sprawling traffic jam to dance atop their cars in a full crayon box of monochromatic dresses or T-shirts. To cajole Mia into stopping by a party that'll end with fireworks and a leap into a pool, her roommates tempt her with a peacock-blue outfit that goes with their gumdrop-tone get-ups. However disappointing the morning after might be, the night feels impossibly thrilling while it's happening.

That's the film's stance on love in a nutshell as well, an ephemeral bliss we pursue knowing all too well that it could leave our hearts mangled. For his parting showstopper, Chazelle raises the ante on Demy's example by showing us the path-not-taken romance that the elder director left implied in pregnant glances. Seb and Mia dash through a montage of the years they could've shared, which deposits them in a Hollywood-ified soundstage Paris—a cheeky full-circle synthesis of the original MGM classics and their adulatory Gallic descendants that takes us back to the backlots where it all started. Our star-crossed lovers can still get a taste of happiness picturing all they lost, just as this film treats us to one last look at the twinkly enchantment of a defunct movement in entertainment, its extravagant colors now fading.

 #809CB0
R128 G156 B176

#E3CD67
R227 G205 B103

 #89453F
R137 G69 B63

#E6C859
R230 G200 B89

#944848
R148 G72 B72

#3F558D
R63 G85 B141

#A0AB7E
R160 G171 B126

#DC965D
R220 G150 B93

#C1C8DD
R193 G200 B221

#5D80AC
R93 G128 B172

#3E518B
R62 G81 B139

A REAL HERO

BLACK PANTHER
RYAN COOGLER
2018

An epidemic of desaturation has swept American studio cinema, leaving a trail of casualties in the blockbusters drained of all visual pep. For those tracking the spread of what film writer Katie Stebbins has termed "intangible sludge," the main offenders are the capes-and-tights-clad moneymakers of the Marvel Cinematic Universe. With their militant adherence to a house style reliant on a fuzziness more easily manipulated during post-production's "color correction" phase, a viewer may feel like they're watching the movie through a limousine's darkened window. This partially explains the exceptional critical embrace of *Black Panther*, a film with a more legible sense of authorship that extends to the pride and purpose with which it wears its colors.

Stopping short of *Dick Tracy*'s maxed-out chromatic anarchy, director Ryan Coogler and cinematographer Rachel Morrison hewed closer to the pizzazz of the comics by turning the lights up on Wakanda, home of the Black Panther superhero born T'Challa. It's an Afrofuturist paradise informed in equal parts by age-old tribal styles and the next-century skyscrapers of Hong Kong or Abu Dhabi, a mix of the traditional and technological also incorporated in Ruth E. Carter's Oscar-winning costuming. The five ruling tribes of

Wakanda broadcast their loyalties through their robes, grouped by color and infused with touches from real-life ethnic groups in Africa. The river-dwelling community wears a boggy green and shells gesturing to the Suri people, the mountain clan dyes their fabric with ocher in the fashion of the Himba, and so on. They wear their clothes like a flag, an assertion of solidarity important in a land with lots of internecine tensions.

The royal family's color-blocking contrasts black against purple, the signifier of vitality for T'Challa's bloodline. His super-suit can absorb damage and shoot it back as purple light, and an elixir made from a purple heart-shaped herb nullifies and restores the superpowers of the Panther. Upon taking it, T'Challa appears on the "ancestral plane," an astral savannah where he communes with his deceased father under a sky filled with violet aurora borealis. Purple is strength, honor, potency, family, legacy; a unifying source of self-empowerment likened to the heritage of Blackness. From under a set of top-down corporate mandates, Coogler got away with something formally distinct that carries his personal themes and preoccupations into the kind of capital-E Entertainment that pairs well with popcorn—y'know, art. It's the story of Hollywood, since time immemorial.

#836699
R131 G102 B153

#2A2639
R42 G38 B57

FIGHT FOR THE RIGHT

LOVERS ROCK
STEVE MCQUEEN
2020

In Rastafari, the Jamaican religion-cum-social movement dedicated to the emancipation of the African diaspora from Western white oppression, adherents hold the colors red, yellow, and green in special esteem. They appeared first on the flag of Ethiopia, an exemplar to those resisting colonialism for its hard-won independence during the period that saw Italian imperialists invading the continent. Red symbolizes the bloodshed of those who died for the cause of freedom, yellow represents gold and the abundant resources of Africa, and green stood in for the fertility of the land. The color scheme pops up all over Steve McQueen's five-film anthology *Small Axe* (so titled for the proverb "small axe fall big tree," later reiterated by Bob Marley and Lee Perry in the chorus to their Rasta anthem of the same name): pins, posters, wool caps, jackets. In "Lovers Rock," the standout of the lot, these colors soak into the visual make-up of the film itself as a strand of political rebellion.

The svelte sixty-eight-minute feature hovers around a house party in West London, a hotspot for the city's robust West Indian population. For young people getting the stink eye from white Brits everywhere they go, social functions like this one are more than a chance to eat homemade curried goat, drink a few Red Stripes, smoke some weed, dance to R&B-inflected reggae, and possibly get lucky. The night is a locus of togetherness, a celebration of Black excellence verging on an act of protest. In the main room, the DJs of Mercury Sound spin their records under the red and yellow lights McQueen mounted overhead to allow for free-roving handheld shooting without fear of anyone being backlit. In addition to setting the mood for the amorous groovers and making the sweaty humidity indoors visible to us, the red/yellow combo (often completed by the green coat of the DJ) reminds everyone that, under the revelry, there's a righteous anger at the injustice outside.

The other color associated with Rastafari is black, used by Jamaican revolutionary Marcus Garvey in his Pan-African activism as a symbol for the skin of his brethren. The most captivating parts of McQueen's palette play upon the faces of his actors, reds and neutral white reflecting off the dewy cheeks and foreheads of the perspiring dancers. For as long as cinema has been around, the predominantly white cinematographers have done a grave disservice to Black actors with lighting and exposure that flattens and simplifies their features, a regrettable sign of an industry apathetic about making room. McQueen and director of photography Shabier Kirchner rebuked this long-standing injury with their painterly pulchritude, de-objectifying the canvas of the Black body.

 #B487B0
R180 G135 B176

#753136
R117 G49 B54

 #92A7C0
R146 G167 B192

#E6B053
R230 G176 B83

#6E4744
R110 G71 B68

FURTHER READING

John Alton, *Painting with Light*,
University of California Press (2013)

Hans P. Bacher and Santan Suryavanshi,
Vision: Color and Composition for Film,
Laurence King Publishing (2018)

Fred E. Basten, *Glorious Technicolor:
The Movies' Magic Rainbow*,
Easton Studio Press (2005)

Patti Bellantoni, *If It's Purple, Someone's
Gonna Die*, Routledge (2005)

David Bordwell, Kristin Thompson and
Jeff Smith, *Film Art: An Introduction*,
McGraw-Hill Education (2020)

Edward Branigan, *Tracking Color
in Cinema and Art: Philosophy and
Aesthetics*, Routledge (2018)

Elizabeth Brayer, *George
Eastman: A Biography*, University
of Rochester Press (2006)

David A. Ellis, *Conversations with
Cinematographers*, Scarecrow Press (2011)

Victoria Finlay, *Color: A Natural
History of the Palette*, Random
House Trade Paperbacks (2002)

Tom Gunning, *Giovanna Fossati,
Joshua Yumibe and Jonathon Rosen,
Fantasia of Color in Early Cinema*,
Amsterdam University Press (2015)

Charles Haine, *Color Grading
101*, Routledge (2019)

Richard W. Haines, *Technicolor
Movies: The History of Dye Transfer
Printing*, McFarland & Co. (2003)

Daan Hertogs and Nico de Klerk, *Disorderly
Order: Colours in Silent Film*, Stichting
Nederlands Filmmuseum (1996)

Scott Higgins, *Harnessing the Technicolor
Rainbow: Color Design in the 1930s*,
University of Texas Press (2007)

Lisa Holewa, *Making Movies in Technicolor*,
Teacher Created Materials (2018)

James Layton and David Pierce,
The Dawn of Technicolor: 1915–1935,
George Eastman House (2015)

Brian McKernan, *Digital Cinema:
The Revolution in Cinematography,
Post-Production, and Distribution*,
McGraw-Hill Education (2005)

Richard Misek, *Chromatic Cinema: A History
of Screen Color*, Wiley-Blackwell (2010)

Sarah Street, Keith M. Johnston, Paul
Frith and Carolyn Rickards, *Colour
Films in Britain: The Eastmancolor
Revolution*, British Film Institute (2021)

Joshua Yumibe, *Moving Color: Early
Film, Mass Culture, Modernism*,
Rutgers University Press (2012)

PICTURE CREDITS

The publisher wishes to thank all those listed below, as well as the film production and distribution companies, for their permission to use the film stills and publicity images reproduced in this book. Every care has been taken to trace copyright holders, but we apologize in advance for any omissions, or neglect, and will be pleased to make any corrections so that a full acknowledgment may be given in subsequent editions.

12 IMDb; 15 Fathom Events/Everett; 19 Wikicommons; 21 Moviestore Collection Ltd/ Alamy; 22–3 Archivio GBB/Alamy; 45 TCD/ Prod.DB/Alamy; 50 Moviestore Collection Ltd/ Alamy; 53 Robert Landau/Alamy; 73–4 TCD/ Prod.DB/Alamy; 77 Dinodia Photos/Alamy; 93 TCD/Prod.DB/Alamy; 94–5t TCD/Prod.DB/ Alamy; 94–5b Collection Christophel/Alamy; 100 Photo 12/Alamy; 103 Lucasfilm/20th Century Fox/Album/Alamy; 106 Landmark Media/Alamy; 115 Moviestore Collection Ltd/ Alamy; 122 Collection Christophel/Alamy; 125 PictureLux/The Hollywood Archive/Alamy; 126 Everett Collection/Alamy; 148 Initial Entertainment Group/Marshak, Bob/Album/ Alamy; 158 Fox 2000 Pictures/Album/Alamy; 161 Pictorial Press Ltd/Alamy; 173 IFC Films/ Everett Collection/Alamy; 174–5t Moviestore Collection Ltd/Alamy; 189 Landmark Media/ Alamy; 191 Landmark Media/Alamy; 199 Parisa Taghizedeh/Amazon/Everett Collection/ Alamy; 201 Parisa Taghizedeh/Amazon/Everett Collection/Alamy.

ACKNOWLEDGMENTS

Special thanks to the superlative team of editors and image hunters—Alice Graham, Joe Hallsworth, Bella Skertchly and John Parton—integral to the conception, creation, and completion of this book, a patient and encouraging bunch who barely even blinked at questions like "Is this blue blue enough?" or "What about the frame with the blood and the eye socket, what do we think of that one?"

For facilitating or otherwise aiding in research, thanks to the Museum of the Moving Image (in particular Eric Hynes and Tomoko Kawamoto), the Musée Méliès at La Cinémathèque Française, the Roxy Cinema (in particular Jon Dieringer), the Criterion Collection and Jordan Hoffman.

And for providing invaluable moral support during the process of writing this book, thanks to cherished friends and complaint-receivers Stephen Schapero, Vikram Murthi, Nick Newman, Mark Asch, Vadim Rizov, and Cady Drell; to my mother Michele and father Clint, who most sensitively heeded my requests that they not ask about my progress on this book, regardless of the undue curtness with which they were delivered; to my sister Eva, who often seems to know me better than I know myself, excepting only the many, many instances in which she has been wrong about everything all the time; and to my dearest darling Maddie, who always talked me down whenever I straddled the brink of hysteria and always said "Bless you" from the next room whenever I sneezed.

INDEX

INDEX

Brimming with creative inspiration, how-to
projects, and useful information to enrich your
everyday life, quarto.com is a favorite destination
for those pursuing their interests and passions.

First published in 2023
by Frances Lincoln,
an imprint of The Quarto Group.
1 Triptych Place,
London, SE1 9SH,
United Kingdom
T (0)20 7700 6700
www.Quarto.com
© 2023 Quarto Publishing Plc
Text © 2023 Charles Bramesco

A catalogue record for this book is
available from the British Library.
ISBN 978-0-7112-7938-4
Ebook ISBN 978-0-7112-7940-7

10 9 8 7 6 5 4 3 2 1

Design by Intercity

Printed in China